M000218492

SITKA SNOW

THE ADVENTURES OF ALASKA'S POLICE CHIEF SNOW AND LILLY

SHELDON SCHMITT

VIRGINIA BEACH
CAPE CHARLES

Sitka Snow:
The Adventures of
Alaska's Police Chief Snow and Lilly

by Sheldon Schmitt

© Copyright 2021 Sheldon Schmitt

ISBN 978-1-64663-556-6

All rights reserved. No part of this publication may be reproduced, stored in a retrieval system, or transmitted in any form or by any means – electronic, mechanical, photocopy, recording, or any other – except for brief quotations in printed reviews, without the prior written permission of the author.

This is a work of fiction. The characters are both actual and fictitious. With the exception of verified historical events and persons, all incidents, descriptions, dialogue and opinions expressed are the products of the author's imagination and are not to be construed as real.

REVIEW COPY: This is an advanced printing subject to corrections and revisions.

Published by

köehlerbooks™

3705 Shore Drive
Virginia Beach, VA 23455
800-435-4811
www.koehlerbooks.com

A portion of the proceeds go to the Alaska Raptor Center in Sitka
alaskaraptor.org

DEDICATION

For my dad and mom,
Bob and Dolores.

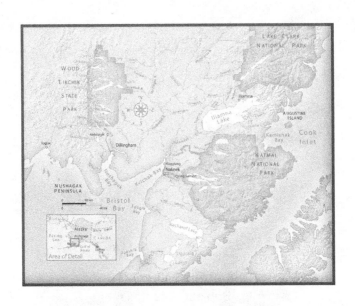

PROLOGUE

BANG!

Snow pulled his sidearm out with his right hand, his left on the seat of the crashed four-wheeler facing him. He heard a shotgun blast and pellets hitting the underside of the machine. Then he heard JJ moan from his pellet wounds. Snow was hit on the left arm, but he didn't think about it, his focus now on finding the culprit. He brought his hands together on the gun and leaned in under the seat of the machine. He was steady as a rock as he acquired his target.

A plane appeared out of nowhere and flew impossibly low, lower than the roof of the shack, and right near Pook. It swooped by in a blur, its wing nearly hitting Pook, who was still standing just out of the doorway of the cabin. The roar was huge as the plane went by. Pook made an animal sound, like *AHHHGG!*

Chubby, the pilot, banked the plane sideways. Pook stood with his gun and followed the plane with it, like he was shooting skeet. He fired a shot, then another at the plane as it banked away.

Chubby thought he may have hit Pook as he made the pass. But no such luck. As he banked away and down toward the beach, he had heard something hitting the plane on the underside. Then again near the tail. He was going to try and set down on the beach, figuring his plane had been shot up.

"Drop the gun!" Snow shouted at Pook, his gun sight trained on Pook's chest. He had him dead to rights.

"Drop the gun!!" Snow shouted again. But Pook had no such intention. He was going to kill Snow. Kill everything.

Pook racked the shotgun and raised it to shoot. Two shots rang out at the same time.

CHAPTER 1
LILLY TAKES A SHOT

Togiak Police Chief Snow was in bed snuggling with Lilly under the covers.

"My favorite time of the day," Snow said to Lilly, and she smiled at him.

One or the other usually said it when they went to bed at night. It was part of their happy routine.

"Yup. Hey, your feet are cold!"

"My feet are always cold," he said.

He draped his legs over hers as they lay facing each other under the heavy quilts. He made a point of putting his cold feet on her legs. She squealed and they both squirmed playfully. She had quick little hands and made him pay.

"Hey, stop it! It was an accident," he lied.

"Yeah, sure," Lilly said, still looking for payback.

"How come your feet are so cold," she said as they calmed a bit and snuggled up.

It was heaven. Lilly had moved in with Chief Snow recently.

She stayed in the Round House when she was in Togiak, working as a nurse for the little clinic. The clinic was part of a larger Bristol Bay health group, so technically she was subject to be moved to wherever staff was needed. But she had some pull, and Togiak could use the help, always. So, she had been granted her request to stay in Togiak on a temporary basis. She was still apt to get recalled to Dillingham or elsewhere in Bristol Bay, but for now she had moved in with Chief Snow.

Lilly was a valued and popular nurse who never complained about the work or travel. She was respected and appreciated by her peers. It was notable that she was accepted in Togiak and other villages, which was not always the case for nurse travelers. Outsiders often felt left out or isolated when working villages. But Lilly's background and experience made those issues mute.

Lilly had been raised in Alaska in a mixture of cultures, primarily Alaska Native. But she was not fully Native. Her mother, who she was close to, was from the Philippines, though her mom was also part White. Her father was Alaska Native. She had learned Tagalog from her mother and her mom's friends when she was a little girl. But she was an Alaska girl and was exposed mostly to her father's culture.

Before moving in with Snow, she had been living with her grandfather, or Oppa, Nikki Wassillie, and his family in Dillingham. Lilly had lived around Alaska and spoke Yupik as did her father and his family. She knew the local ways and language, which was part of the reason she seemed to be quickly accepted in places like Togiak, where locals usually were very slow to embrace outsiders. The other part for her acceptance in the bush was simply Lilly. People quickly warmed to her. Lilly had a remarkable ability to be direct with people but in such a way that they did not get angry or defensive.

As Lilly and Snow were frolicking under the sheets, they heard the unmistakable sound of a shotgun blast at close range. The sounds of glass shattering and the shot hitting the side of the house came directly after the discharge. Lilly looked at him and said, "Go!"

Snow scrambled out of bed and grabbed his gun belt from the top of the dresser and slung it over his shoulder. He ran to the front door of the house in his boxers and white T-shirt. He slipped his sidearm out of the holster and tossed the gun belt on the green and red couch near the door.

He opened the door to the arctic entry and saw the glass window on top of the outer door was blown out. He sidled carefully over the glass, his Nike flip flops crunching bits of glass under foot. It was cold in the entryway.

"Come out here, Snow, you little fucker!" James Pook hollered.

"You don't belong in Togiak! You can either get out, or I'm gonna shoot you! Get out here, fucking gussock cop!" Pook practically spit the word *gussock*, which was a derogatory term for white people used by the locals. The term originally came from the Russian *cossack*.

Snow was under cover in the entry at the right side of the door. He was in the shadows of the entryway and peeked out at Pook, who was swaying and appeared plenty drunk. Pook was cradling the shotgun casually in his arms, the barrel nestled in the crook of his left arm, the right holding the stock. He was leaning against the rear rack of a Honda ATV, or four-wheeler as most locals called them.

■ ■ ■

Pook was a big man by local standards, standing at about five foot ten inches and stocky strong. Snow once felt his force in a wrestling match against him, arresting him during another of his alcohol fueled rampages.

On that day this past summer, Pook had been in rare form. He drank a jug he got from his niece but wanted more. He *knew* she had more "boosh," the local way of saying booze. He went to her place and threatened harm unless she told him where the boosh was. When she told him she did not have any more, he went to the artic entry, or cunny chuck, and grabbed a shot gun. He came back in and pointed it at her and hollered, "Where's the rest of your jugs, bitch! Tell me!!"

She told him and ran out the back door, her little kids hot on her heels. She practically flew the block or so to the yellow tin shack that was the police department and ran inside, her two kids huddled around her as she told Snow what happened. Stanley Beans was there that day, in the office just shooting the breeze with Snow when the niece ran in with the kids. She was terrified as she told them her story. The kids, literally shaking, melted into their mom for protection. Snow saw Beans' eyes were big behind his black framed glasses with the smeared coke bottle lens.

It was weird how it all happened so fast that day. Immediately after taking her statement, he looked out the front window and saw Pook stalking the school playground. He did not appear to have a long gun with him.

"You stay here," Snow said calmly to the mom and kids.

"Stanley come with me. I need you to drive the truck." Beans looked like he wanted no part of this, shaking his head as if to say, *no no no.*

"I just need you to drive, that's it. I'm gonna jump out and deal with Pook. Come on, we're going now," Snow said reassuringly, gently pulling Beans with him toward the door. Beans was still shaking his head but did as he was told.

Faithful volunteer jail guard and deputy wannabe Stanley Beans drove the beat up white three-quarter-ton pickup toward the school playground where Pook was walking purposefully. Snow now saw that his scared waif of a wife was walking with him. The time elapsed was only a minute or two since the young niece came into the station.

Snow instructed Beans to drive past Pook fifty feet or so, and he slid from the truck as it was still rolling to a stop. He quickly assessed Pook. He saw no visible weapons; he was wearing a light jacket and a menacing look.

Snow said, "James Pook, stop, man. You are under arrest for assault." No sense beating around the bush. Snow put out his arm like he was stopping traffic and said, "stop," again. Snow was in his path, but Pook didn't slow. Snow pushed his outstretched hand into Pook's barrel chest, Pook slapped at it.

"Get the fuck out of my path, little snowflake!" Pook virtually spit the words. But Snow wasn't going anywhere, and the confrontation immediately sparked.

Pook came at Snow and took a vicious swing at his head. Snow saw it coming and ducked just in time as the blow glanced off the top of his head. Snow ducked under and behind Pook, who was angry and strong, but drunk and slow. Snow knew that drunks don't lose strength, only mobility. He was behind and curled his leg around Pook's leg and tripped him to the frozen gravel, landing on top of him with as much force as possible, hoping to stun the big man. But Pook seemed unfazed.

The ground fight lasted only a few minutes but seemed to Snow like forever. Pook kept trying to get a hold of the police chief and grabbed, fought, kicked, and generally struggled in vain to get up. Snow kept working him from behind, keeping him down, switching sides, and reapplying force when needed to keep him mostly on the ground. They were both tiring, and Snow kept repeating, "Stop fighting." Verbal warnings ignored, Snow gave Pook a shot of pepper spray in the face, but it didn't really seem to do anything. *Too close.* Pepper spray needed some space to properly get airborne to be inhaled. At very close range, the yellow-orange spray simply wets and sticks to the skin, not airborne enough to vaporize and get in the eyes or lungs to do what was intended.

Pook finally stopped, panted, and seemed spent. Then he laughed.

"You little shit!" said Pook.

Snow cuffed him. After the fight was over, Pook was laughing and in a good mood. *People are weird*, Snow thought.

Pook had gone to trial and lost. He got about two years for pointing the gun at his niece. He ended up only doing about six months, though, for a variety of reasons, including good behavior. *Hard to believe the good behavior,* Snow had thought.

■ ■ ■

Pook had only been out for about six months or so. But here he was again, armed, dangerous, and threatening.

"James! Put down the gun before someone gets hurt!" Snow shouted into the night.

"*Eeeee!* Fuck you, Snow!" Pook hollered and racked the shotgun. He fired a shot in the general direction of the front door, hitting a few feet above. The blast seemed impossibly loud; smoke drifting away from the muzzle of the long gun, easily visible in the night, with the soft glow of a streetlight backlighting the scene. The gun smoke drifted over the four-wheeler. *No wind,* part of Snow's mind whispered.

Pook racked the shotgun again as he hollered, "Come on, Snow! Come out here!"

Snow saw a small flash and heard a snap from his left.

What the hell, Lilly.

"*Aghhhh!* You shot me, you little bastard!"

Well, someone did, thought Snow, but it wasn't me. *Lilly, what in the hell are you doing?* thought Snow. He had been keeping his eyes down range but now snuck a peek over at Lilly. Lilly had magically slipped into place to his left without Snow seeing or sensing her presence. She could do that; sometimes she seemed to move like a ghost.

Her eyes were locked on Pook, but she acknowledged Snow's peek at her with a quick nod. *She's impossibly beautiful even in this moment,* thought Snow. *Especially in this moment,* he amended.

"That's how you shoot someone in the leg. You don't have to kill'em . . . just shoot'em in the leg," Lilly said quietly, with finality, like this was a statement of fact and not something to be debated. It was her way.

Snow chewed on her statement as he prepared to act. He didn't know she could shoot and had never even seen her handle a gun. She was an Alaska girl, though. Many of them knew how to shoot, hunt, gut a moose, or filet a fish. Many could handle a boat or operate a four-wheel drive truck. So, it shouldn't have been a big surprise. But it was.

Snow kept thinking of Lilly as a kind of fragile flower. Beautiful, but not the rough and tough tobacco chewing, cussing, and spitting typical hot Alaska chick. He had to admit, he was dead wrong about her, or at least that she was full of surprises. She was dainty and soft spoken but was also frontier rugged. Snow couldn't help but think her comment about shooting someone in the leg was probably subtle commentary about his own shooting ability—or lack thereof. He was going to have to get her out to the dump and see what she could do with a pistol. *If we got out of this,* the other side of his brain interjected.

Lilly had slipped on her dark red parka and mukluk style slippers over her pajamas. The parka hood was pulled up and the wolf ruff framed her head. Tendrils of her black-as-raven hair poked out from the hood. She had his black plastic stock .22 long rifle against her right shoulder. She was using the door jamb as a rest for her left hand, which also held the front grip.

Pook had plopped onto the ground. He was sitting in the road in the snow and gravel, with his hand clutching his right thigh, his shotgun in the snow a few feet away.

"You hit me in the bone!" hollered Pook. "The bone!"

"I'm going out, Lilly. Cover me," Snow said.

His parka was right there in the entry, so he grabbed it and slid it on, keeping an eye on Pook who sat up.

Snow had his duty weapon, his Glock Model 21 forty caliber sidearm in his right hand with his left as support. He had the gun in the guard position, meaning it was pointed lower toward the ground.

Snow had noticed that in extremely stressful moments such as the one he was in, his mind seemed to split and be entirely capable of concentrating on more than one thing at once. It even seemed as though his mental compartments would hold conversations with one another. It was an odd thing, but one that Snow had experienced before. So, it came as no surprise when part of his mind was wondering about Lilly, even in this moment with James Pook on the ground. Snow marveled at that fact that she could handle a firearm and remained calm in this stressful situation. He wondered what else there was about Lilly that he did not know.

Snow carefully crept toward Pook. The shotgun was close enough for Pook to reach, and Snow wanted to be prepared.

"James, I want to get you some help. Get that wound treated," Snow stated in a normal conversational voice. "The clinic is right across the street. Let me get you over there so they can take a look at your leg."

Pook seemed focused on his leg.

"Jesus, I was just fooling around. You didn't have to shoot me. I mean you hit me in the bone. I'm gonna have to go to Dillingham to get this fixed!" Pook said, calmer now, even sad. "Godammit, right in the bone," he said under his breath, like he might cry.

"Yah, probably. We'll see what the health aide has to say when she looks at it," Snow said as he picked up the shotgun. He quickly put the gun in the front seat of his battered white Isuzu SUV, one of his "police vehicles". He had two, both near the end of their lifespan.

He holstered his gun and came back to Pook.

As he knelt beside Pook, he noticed Lilly was standing now about five feet away, holding her small rifle purposefully. She had again slipped into position without either Snow or Pook noticing her. She still had the rifle up to her shoulder, in the ready position, looking perfectly comfortable and confident. Despite the cold, Lilly had pulled her hood down, as she wanted to be able to clearly see all around the perimeter now that she was in the open.

"What the fuck! You shot me, Lilly! You did, didn't you?" Pook spit at Lilly in a kind of whiny voice as he held his leg. Snow tried to keep Pook's attention on his leg, and off Lilly.

Snow noticed Stanley Beans coming toward them from the direction of town. *Thank God, some help*, he thought.

"Lilly, you little bitch! What in the fuck you shoot me for?! I am going to totally fuck you up, little woman. I'll take that pea shooter and shove it up your pee peet!" Pook threatened, using a slang term for a woman's parts.

"Try it. I got more bullets. I coulda shot your pecker, but I didn't, but I can if you want," Lilly barked. Pook's look of shock, surprise, and anger was priceless to Snow. Pook's face was screwed up into a twist and his lips were pursed like he was going to say something, but Lilly had cut him to the quick.

She had a dish towel in her left hand that was still under the front of the gun. She raised the barrel and casually tossed the towel to Snow who snatched it with his right hand.

Jeez Lilly, you're cold as ice, thought Snow, the cop in him respecting Lilly's cool, calm demeanor under pressure.

Snow used the distractions to check Pook for any other weapons in his coat or belt. He found a box of shells in Pook's jacket pocket that he quickly slid in his own parka pocket. Otherwise, Pook was clean, so to speak.

"James, lift your hands so I can put this towel on your leg," Chief Snow said quietly.

"Snow, you better get your bitch on a leash!" Pook slurred, finally addressing what was clearly on his mind.

"Owwww! Damn, that hurts!" Pook winced. *Dang, he's whiney*, thought Snow. *It's just a little bullet hole.*

"Stanley, start up my four-wheeler, would ya?" Snow said to his friend, jail guard, and all-around helper. Even though he had the truck, Snow knew he did not want to wait for it to warm up. The four-wheeler was quicker; you could start it and go.

"Eeeee," Stanley said, the local way of saying "yes" or "okay."

Pook's leg was barely bleeding; the bullet hole in his pants looked small. Bitter cold seemed to slow bleeding. Snow thought it might be true that the bullet hit the bone, as it was lined up that way.

"What the hell were you doing shooting like that, James? You coulda kilt someone, ya know?" Snow said to Pook as he prepared to get him up.

"Ah, Shit. I only meant to scare you. I didn't know your little house mouse would shoot me," Pook laughed. "Jesus, Snow. I mean really, tell Lilly to put the gun down, would ya?" Then in an angry voice, "Lilly, you're gonna get yours, little girl! I promise you that!" Pook shouted.

Lilly had lowered the gun but still looked ready for action.

The four-wheeler was running now, and Snow motioned to Pook that he would help him up.

"Hey, Snow, help me up, would ya?" Pook said, now sounding friendly, like he and Snow were old friends.

"Gotta put these on, James," Snow said and slipped on the cuffs without waiting for an answer. "I gotta charge you with shooting up my place, but we're going to the clinic, not the jail."

"You know some people call you *Schnauzer*, Snow, cause you're kinda like one of those mean little dogs," Pook said with a laugh.

"I think it fits, ya know . . . Schnauzer! Ha ha!" Pook slurred and laughed. Pook's wild mood swings were not surprising to Chief Snow, and, in fact, were common for drunks. Snow thought, *Great, a shitty nickname after a little yippy dog. Hope it doesn't stick.*

Stanley Beans had come to help and one lawman on each side helped Pook up. Snow had ripped the towel in half and tied it around the wound on Pook's leg. Together, they all hobbled over to the four-wheeler and Pook plopped onto the back rack of the ATV.

"Meet you at the clinic, Stanley. Thanks, brother," Snow said with genuine affection. Stanley's eyebrows fluttered, and he smiled, showing a gap between his front teeth, his eyes twinkling behind his black frame eyeglasses.

"Eeeee, Chief."

CHAPTER 2
THE VILLAGE

"Lilly, I didn't even know you could shoot a gun."

"Of course I can, silly," Lilly said, rolling her eyes. "I learned to shoot when I was little. I used to practice shooting at cans and stuff. I am a good shot."

"Were you aiming for that spot?"

"Eeee, of course, silly."

Beans entered the small and grungy police station. Snow looked around at the scene. There had been a lot of activity since Lilly shot James Pook in the leg. It was nice to have some company, for sure. Two Alaska troopers had come in to investigate the shooting, which had gone smoothly. Trooper Dick Dikron and Trooper Debbie Roop were assigned to the area around Dillingham. Just two troopers to cover a dozen villages or so, some of them sizable and with little or no other law enforcement.

Togiak was a village of about 900 people, 90 percent of whom were Alaska Native. It was the biggest and busiest village in the district, warranting a full-time police chief and a jail keeper. Most villages had one police officer, or none at all. It was a complicated patchwork that left Bush Alaska with limited and stretched law enforcement coverage. Often the officers they had in the bush were part-time and under-trained. Those local officers were complimented by a blanket of state trooper coverage. But the troopers were stretched thin too and were often posted in one of the hubs and were not always available to help out in a crisis. It was not uncommon for a trooper to arrive a day or so after an event. That was just a fact of life living out in Bush Alaska.

The villages in Alaska were vastly different than small towns in the lower forty-eight. There was much more crime than similarly sized towns down in the world. Lots of alcohol fueled crimes of violence. And most of the villages, like Togiak, were not accessible by road. It made for a kind of Wild West atmosphere.

The two troopers had made the trip over for the shooting at Chief Snow's request. He felt it was best to have an outside agency investigate the shooting so there was no room for anyone to claim that he had sat on the investigation or smothered it because of Lilly's involvement.

Troopers Dick and Debbie were extraordinarily capable people, and Snow considered them friends. The feeling was mutual. They were still in Togiak wrapping up things, though they had stepped out to grab some food or something.

Stanley Beans was an unusual man and hard to characterize. He could be obtuse at times, a dull look clouding his eyes, the impression being that the computer was temporarily frozen. He would often sputter a bit, then jerk to life, like a four-wheeler with some bad gas.

Aside from the two troopers, Snow relied most heavily on his sidekick, Stanley Beans, technically a jail guard, but more like a deputy to the chief. Stanley and his older brother, Frank N Beans, had migrated down from the Bethel area up north to Bristol Bay some years ago for work. Stanley was very slender and about five feet five or so, much taller than his brother. Stanley wore black jeans and white bunny boots, despite the weather warming up. Today, he donned a well-worn black parka and a black ball cap above his jet-black hair. His most distinctive feature was the black-frame glasses, which accentuated the largeness of his eyes. The term bug-eyed came to mind for many villagers when describing him.

Stanley was about forty-something years old, and it was hard to say and easy to underestimate his age given his sometimes childlike behavior. But he was smart and intuitive, often surprising Snow. Most importantly to the chief, Stanley was loyal.

"Eeee, most Native women are good shots. They have small hands," Stanley said in his deliberative singsong manner, peppered with the local term *Eeee,* which meant agreement usually, but which could also mean a lot more depending on the inflection.

"Police department" was a loose description of the yellow metal shack that stood in the middle of the village across the street from the all-grades school building. The police department appeared to be under construction or renovation, but that was an illusion. It was as good as it was going to get, and the ladder propped up against the side of the building, or the half-finished tile floor symbolized the rustic nature of living in these isolated communities.

In the back country, most jobs were finished when you ran out of tile, paint, tools, or energy. And then that half-finished job joined the long list of other incomplete ambitions on display in the village. Life in the bush was like that. To outsiders, if felt incomplete, disheveled, and even Third World.

"Small hands? Let me see your hands, Lilly; you too, Stanley."

Lilly edged closer to where Snow was standing, his usual spot by the nearly exhausted Bunn coffee maker. A suspect can of condensed milk with two misshapen holes poked in the top was nearby, in case of a bad coffee emergency.

Lilly moved closer without seeming to move her feet, kind of like floating to Snow with her tiny hand in the air. Stanley clumped over and held up his remarkably dirty hands complete with black grime under his nails. His hands were almost dainty and not much larger than Lilly's. Snow held up his right hand to match up with Lilly. His hand was almost half again as big as hers. Then he put his hand over and matched it up with Stanley's.

"Based on your theory, you should be a good shot too, Stanley, but we both know you are almost as bad as me," Snow joked.

"Eeee, my left leg is shorter than my right leg," Stanley said.

Snow and Lilly turned to stare at Stanley, who suddenly looked uneasy.

"It's always been that way," Stanley said.

Snow was going to remark at the wonder of Stanley Beans' shorter left leg affecting his ability to shoot straight but thought better of it. He did not want to hurt the feelings of his friend.

"You should put a quarter in your left boot, Stanley. It will help you shoot better," said Lilly, with a smile that would melt butter.

"Really? I will try it, Lilly!" Stanley said with excitement in his voice.

"*Salamat*, Lilly!" Stanley surprisingly said in Tagalog, the Philippine language.

Snow smiled as he again held up his hand toward Lilly. Instead of putting her hand up to match his again, she playfully slapped it away. Both Lilly and Chief Snow smiled.

All the drama of the shooting had passed, and life was returning to normal in Togiak, Alaska.

"Are you my deputy now?" Snow asked Lilly.

"I can teach you how to shoot. But I already got a job working at the clinic," Lilly remarked. She could handle the give and take with the boys, no doubt about it. She gave as good as she got.

Lilly enjoyed being with the boys at the police shack. It was exciting and she always felt welcome. Despite her naturally demure ways, she was a social person and liked the camaraderie and joking that was standard fare at the local cop shop. She also liked to be close to her lover. And she was protective toward him. She adjusted her parka a bit to let in some air as it was getting warm in the station. Lilly looked around at the surroundings and thought the place needed a good cleaning.

She looked down past the fur ruff at the bottom of her deep red parka down to the floor. She was standing on battered off white tile, but about half the floor was bare plywood. She spotted an open box of floor tile in the corner and wondered why the job had been abandoned. She sidled over and with one finger lifted the lid and looked inside the box. The floor tiles in the box looked to be a different size and style. The top floor tile in the box was broken. She let the lid slide off her finger and it flopped back down.

The tile and plywood floor were strewn with a mix of sand and small rocks of various sizes. Togiak was a sand and rock kind of place. The large main room in the office served as a meeting place, a kitchen of sorts, a booking area for the two jail cells, and a couple ancient looking metal desks of World War II vintage. Old but very sturdy.

She looked over at Snow. *He's so handsome,* she thought, *but no pretty boy.* He was wearing blue overalls over top of a blue police uniform shirt. The overalls were dusty and looked like they needed to be washed. His black police boots were scuffed and also needed attention. His skin was brown, and hair was dark with eyes to match. He needed a shave. She wondered for the hundredth time if he was a white man or exactly what racial mix? Lilly had asked Snow in the past, but it seemed that he was unsure of his real roots because he was adopted.

Snow caught Lilly checking him out and flashed a coy smile. She looked away and her face flushed a bit.

"Brady, this place is dirty, needs a good cleaning. You too!" she said.

Brady. Stanley kind of half silently mouthed the name as his eyebrows went up. No one ever used the chief's first name; everyone referred to him as Chief Snow or simply Chief.

"You are welcome to do some cleaning anytime, Deputy Lilly Wassillie," Snow joked. "The cleaning supplies are in the closet there by the bathroom. Deputy Beans will happily assist you." Stanley snorted into his coffee, giving a look that he would do no such thing. *Chief must be joking,* he thought.

"I am not joking, Stanley," Chief Snow said, reading Stanley's look.

The truth of the matter is that it was extremely difficult to keep anything clean. The roads there were all a mixture of sand, mud, and rocks. The entire village was built on sand and rocks; things were always dusty or muddy, and remarkably often both at the same time.

The village was about a hundred air miles southwest from the major hub that was Dillingham, Alaska. There were no roads in or out of Togiak. You either flew in or arrived by boat. In Alaska, they called it "off the road system," as most of the villages in Alaska were off the road.

The village proper sat right on the mouth of the river at the confluence of the Togiak River, which flowed into Togiak Bay. In the distance toward the south, you could see the wonderful Walrus Islands on the waters of Bristol Bay. These islands were the home of a wonderful and mysterious event. Each year, thousands of walruses would hit the beach or *haul out* on the islands. On the beach, they would seem to just hang out and do walrus things. No one seemed to know exactly why the walruses chose to haul out on the beach near Togiak.

The village sat on the west side of the river mouth, most of the town stretched out right on the riverbank. Across the river was the very small village of Twin Hills. There was a cannery across the river that opened and functioned in the summer, when the huge Bristol Bay salmon fishery was in full swing.

■ ■ ■

The door of the police station flew open and was filled with the formidable presence of Sergeant Dick Dickron. He filled up the doorway and stood there for a bit before entering. Most people called him Trooper Dick, or simply Big Dick. He cut an impressive figure in his pressed blue uniform, with a crisp crease in the trousers, and topped with the blue campaign hat complete with a gold braid. He was perhaps six feet two or a bit more. *He must be a very imposing figure, if he was bearing down on you,* thought Snow. Everything about him seemed squared away.

He strode into the room and over to the coffee pot. Snow accidently bumped into his stomach as he moved away from the coffee pot. *God, his stomach is like a rock,* thought Snow.

"Please be careful with that thing," Snow said, pointing at Trooper Dick's gut. "It's like a dangerous weapon."

Trooper Dick ignored the comment. Trading jabs was how they often communicated. They sparred with words.

Trooper Debbie Roop had entered behind Trooper Dick. People called her Trooper Debbie. She was as small as Trooper Dick was large. She had strawberry tendrils sticking out from under her trooper hat. She had on a blue parka that hung to her knees. She was forty something, and smart as a whip. She had freckles on her nose and was pretty, but tough. Snow had seen her handle drunks twice her size, with apparent ease. *She was going places,* thought Snow.

"Got the medical report," Trooper Dick announced to the room. "You did get him in the bone, Lilly. The bullet is stuck there; it never came out!"

"Wow, good shot, Lilly! You aiming for the bone?" Trooper Debbie asked with a smile.

Lilly smiled, her perfect white teeth on display.

"Nope. Just aimed for the middle of his thigh. Had to stop him before he killed someone," Lilly said, and shot a glance at Snow.

"You should go to the range with me sometime, Lilly, so we can shoot together. Dang good shot that was!" Trooper Dick said. He had been standing near Lilly and reached over and put his arm around her and drew her into him. She reached her arms and gave him a warm embrace. Chief Snow felt a pang of jealousy, which he quickly repressed.

"My bone, you shot me in the BONE!" Trooper Debbie said, mocking James Pook and grabbing at her thigh. "YOU SHOT ME IN THE BONE!"

"I can shoot your pecker if you want. I got some more bullets!" Trooper Debbie mocked, imitating what Lilly had said to Pook.

They all had a laugh at Pook's expense. Snow noticed that Trooper Dick still had his arm over Lilly's shoulder. *Take if off!* thought Snow.

"Maybe I could come with when you go shoot, pick up some pointers," said Snow hopefully. The chief did not actually like going to shoot; he only did so to keep his skills sharp, so to speak. He never really liked going out to shoot. It was just part of the job, but he took no enjoyment out of it.

Trooper Debbie sidled up to Snow and said with some hot sauce and a wink, "I surely can give you some pointers, Chief."

"What in the *fuck* is that?" Trooper Dick huffed. By dropping the f-bomb, he was officially announcing recess for the children.

"Hey, he's single, and I'm single and highly desirable," Trooper Debbie said with a sultry smile and her hand on her hip. She put her hand on Snow's chest, coquettishly. Snow grew nervous as hell.

"Ah . . . I got a GF," Snow stammered. He moved over a bit and put his arm around Lilly, intentionally knocking Trooper Dick's arm away.

"Girlfriend," Snow said.

"I was thinking of another meaning of GF," Trooper Debbie said. Then she laughed, breaking character.

"You can have him!" Lilly said, joining in the play. "He's not house broken," she teased. "Besides, I kinda like Deputy Beans!" she said, moving over to where Stanley was sitting, placing her hand on his shoulder in a mock gesture of affection.

"Don't worry, it will be our secret, Stanley Hot Beans!" Lilly gushed.

Stanley looked about to have a core melt down.

"I got no secrets!" he said, pleading to Chief Snow. "My left leg is shorter than my right leg!" he blurted out. "Not exactly a great catch."

Everyone laughed at Stanley's comment, but he just wanted to disappear. He didn't like that kind of mocking attention.

"We gotta quit coming over here to save your ass, Snow!" Trooper Dick said to Snow, only half joking.

"Ah, you love it," Snow responded.

"I just wanted to see Lilly, anyway, make sure she's all right, or needs anything," Trooper Dick said.

"First real thing you said all day," Snow remarked.

"You got things wrapped up?" Snow asked in the direction of Trooper Debbie.

She was the brains of the operation and Trooper Dick was the brawn and had a ton of experience. But he could be like a sledgehammer at times. Trooper Debbie was very smart and subtle. She kind of guided investigations or operations when Trooper Dick was bulldozing too far off in one direction or another. Snow often thought she was destined for big things. *Anyone who can handle big Dick like she can is going places,* Snow thought, smiling at the double entendre.

"Yup. Got all the statements, and now a med report. Everything is neat and tidy. James Pook will be charged with reckless endangerment and MIW for being in possession of a firearm while under the influence," Trooper Debbie said, easily shifting into legal lingo.

"Drunk with a gun," Chief Snow and Trooper Dick said at the same time. Cops always liked to say, *drunk with a gun*.

"You work well together, you two,'" Snow said, waving his hand in the direction of the troopers. "I mean, you are good with Big Dick," the chief smirked at Trooper Debbie.

"That counts you out!" she said, smiling back.

"Burn!" Lilly scoffed with a smile and Trooper Dick smiled at her. Trooper Dick really was smitten by Lilly, but who could blame him?

"I gotta go now. Do something," Stanley said, still looking mighty uncomfortable. He stood.

"Us too," Trooper Dick said, looking at Trooper Debbie. "Back to work. Go fire up our chariot." Play time was over.

"You have a council meeting, Chief, don't forget!" Stanley reminded Snow. It was already past time for the council meeting to start, but things always started late in Togiak. Village time.

That's my cue, thought Chief Snow.

"You want a ride home?" Snow asked Lilly.

"No, I am walking, thanks!" Stanley responded. Snow and Lilly exchanged lusty glances.

"I could use a ride to the clinic, Brady," Lilly said. Stanley looked over at Snow with eyebrows raised as if to say, *That okay calling you that, Chief?*

Snow shot Stanley a look, a grimace back as if to say, *Nope only Lilly calls me Brady.*

"Okay, Lilly, let's go, we're burning daylight," Snow said, using a phrase he picked up from his favorite pilot, Chubby Libbits. Everyone left the station together.

■ ■ ■

Snow hopped onto his Honda ATV four-wheeler parked right outside the police shack. He stood on the pegs allowing Lilly room to mount up behind him. Driving a four-wheeler was pretty much Snow's favorite thing to do, preferring it to driving the two battered vehicles that served as the police patrol units. The ATV started immediately, and they were at the front door to the clinic in a minute.

Lilly got off and started to move toward the steps.

"Hey! Come here, aren't you forgetting something?" Snow said.

Lilly turned and Snow could see by her smile that she was messing with him.

Each parting seemed painful, but with the happy prospect of seeing each other again soon.

Snow looked around, then grabbed Lilly and gave her a quick embrace. Lilly pushed back at him, but halfheartedly, and then seemed to pull him in. Snow gave her a kiss on the cheek, which seemed like the thing to do in public.

He was still getting used to the idea of having a GF; he was still guarded.

After Lilly came into his life, he realized how lonely he had been. It seemed the whole world had changed, things had more color now, food tasted better. He worried less about little things. It turns out, he had never really been in love before.

"Love you," he whispered into the raven black hair covering her ear. He could smell her hair and it smelled good.

"You do? I thought I was just convenient," she said back to him with a smile.

"See you after the meeting," Snow said to Lilly.

Snow did a 180 and was heading back in the other direction before Lilly had even made it into the clinic.

■ ■ ■

Snow braked hard and hopped off the four-wheeler while it was still rocking. He managed to beat the cloud of dust that was following him as he stepped through the door to the city offices where the council meeting was being held.

As he entered, he was immediately confronted by Smalley, a mentally handicapped man who spent most of his time patrolling the village in search of coffee and cigarettes.

"Coffee?" Smalley asked, a fingerprint smeared fruit jar in his hand extended toward the chief.

"Sure, Smalley," Snow responded, taking the jar and heading over to the beat-up Bunn coffee maker, virtually identical to the one in the police station. Just different dents.

Chief Snow wondered why Smalley did not just get his own coffee from the pot but figured he had probably been chastised before for doing so. He would stand in one spot for fifteen to thirty minutes waiting for someone to arrive so he could ask for coffee.

Snow poured some brew into the jar and added some water, which was the procedure, and handed it back to Smalley.

"Smoke?" Smalley asked.

Snow had anticipated this and was already fishing the Marlboros out of his pocket. He handed Smalley a couple smokes and he was out the door before Chief Snow had the pack back in the top left pocket of his blue overalls.

He walked into the meeting room and was surprised to see the meeting appeared to be already in session. A meeting starting on time in the village was a rarity. There were four rectangular tables pushed together, and council members already seated looked up at Snow as he entered and took a seat at the table. He noticed Charlie Johnson sitting in one of the chairs along the wall reserved for spectators. Snow tilted his head back as a sign of recognition toward Charlie who did the same.

Charlie Johnson was the most enigmatic person Snow had ever known. He was, until recently, the one person the chief was most worried about having to square off against in the village. He was a fisherman of some renown, a reputation that included fishing illegally, a so-called "creek robber." He was also, until recently, one of the major bootleggers in the village, and certainly had a reputation as a drinker and brawler. He once bit a man's eyebrow off. Snow had seen the scar and tiny remnant of eyebrow still in place on the man who had lost it.

Charlie had a life force about him that was extraordinary. He seemed more alive than other people. He had an urgency about him that could be construed as arrogance. And it was certainly true that he could be cocky as well, but he simply had an animalistic quality that drew in some and was off-putting to others. To top it off, he had a certain animosity toward outside folks and was a Native rights activist. It made no difference that he was half white, which, in fact, perhaps, made him more passionate.

Last year, Charlie Johnson had saved Chief Snow's life. Snow had gotten into a life-or-death struggle with Buck Nelson and was losing the fight. He felt like he was about to lose everything when Charlie appeared out of nowhere and clanged a shovel on Buck's back. That gave Snow a chance to get out from under and grab his gun. Moments later, he shot and killed Buck Nelson, who had lurched at him with a knife.

There was some mystery involved in this relationship and this incident. When Snow asked Charlie Johnson about his sudden and fortuitous appearance, he explained it this way:

"Kinka of the Little People told me I needed to get up here, that you were gonna need saving. So, I came, and sure enough . . ."

"Makes sense," Chief Snow had said, knowing that it sounded crazy. But it was all true. He knew so because Kinka of the Little People had saved his life after he had been attacked by a bear.

"Kinka said we have the same father. We are half-brothers," Charlie said that day.

Everything changed between them after that day. And Charlie seemed to change his ways, at least for a bit. Snow was glad Charlie had taken a reprieve from bootlegging and poaching, but being a cynical chief, he remained skeptical Charlie would stay on the straight and narrow.

■ ■ ■

It turns out, the council had been talking about Snow and his GF when he sat to join them.

"I like Lilly Wassillie. I hear she is a good nurse. We can certainly use her here. At the clinic. Her family are good people; I know her Oppa," said Mayor Moses.

Mayor Moses was a man among men. A hawk nosed light skinned Native who was mayor for good reason. He wore the mantle of leadership as comfortably as an old pair of worn deck slippers.

"Well, I think it is a good thing that the chief has a girlfriend. It's too lonely to be a police chief without a woman. It's a hard job, you know," said Councilwoman Annie Blue.

"Well, besides being a nurse, it seems like she is also a pretty good shot," said Mayor Moses dryly. Everyone chuckled.

Chief Snow's mouth had dropped, but he remained silent.

"I approve of Chief Snow having a girlfriend and think it's a positive thing. Even if they are not married yet," said Annie Blue.

Chief Snow blushed and shook his head. *Approve?*

Charlie Johnson leaned forward in his chair and clapped Snow on the back, a bit too hard, making it sting. Chief Snow shot him an irritated look and mouthed, "Ow" as he rubbed the spot Charlie had smacked.

"She's a better shot than Chief Snow, that's certain! But that's not saying much," said Charlie. "She can teach you how to shoot maybe. When you gonna propose, Chief?" Charlie asked, squeezing the soft spot between Snow's shoulder and neck, hard enough to make him wince.

Chief Snow turned his head away from the others to face directly at Charlie behind him. He mouthed the words *fuck you* at Charlie. Then he mouthed it again just to make sure he got it. Charlie smiled his big wolfish smile, raised his eyebrows, and said, "Eeee," meaning he got it and appreciated it!

Chief Snow turned back to the table and tilted his head to one side with a pained look. But he was determined not to engage or say anything to the council. He knew they were teasing him for a little live entertainment. *Busting chops for fun,* he thought. But he also sensed there was something more at play, a kind of vetting of the new person in town, and her relationship with their employee, Chief Snow. He did not want to give them the satisfaction of commenting or getting into a discussion about his personal life.

"Eeee. You need to start having kids, but first you gotta marry Lilly. Charlie's right about that," said Annie Blue. Chief Snow really liked Annie Blue. She was a Tribal court judge and very wise, but she was getting under his skin at this moment, even if she was a respected Elder.

"You can chase Lilly around in circles in the Round House!" Mayor Moses joked, referring to the old wood stave water tank Chief Snow lived in. It was indeed round, and, in fact, everyone called it the Round House. Chief Snow had a very brief R rated vision of chasing Lilly around the Round House.

"I think it's a good thing to be married; it settles you down," said Mayor Moses to Chief Snow, seemingly unwilling to let this go. "Lilly is a keeper. Not sure what she sees in the chief, though," he laughed.

Almost imperceptibly, Snow cracked a small and pained smile, more like a grimace, really. He just wanted it all to stop now.

"So, it's settled. We all approve of the chief having a girlfriend. At this point, I would normally make a motion, but I think it's not necessary cause Chief and Lilly will be making plenty motions!" Mayor Moses joked. Everyone laughed except Chief Snow, though he did appreciate the joke.

The council returned to regular business, sensing that Chief Snow had received enough ribbing for one night. Just as they were about to start another discussion, Charlie piped in.

"I am here to announce I am running for council," he said. Everyone knew Charlie was a potential leader to rival Mayor Moses.

"There are so many things we need to work on, but tonight I want to talk about a young girl who is missing. Mary Frank went to Anchorage on medical but has disappeared there," Charlie said.

Charlie talked for a bit about how this disappearance was not the first time villagers went missing in Anchorage, and in fact was a pattern they were all too familiar with. They would go to Anchorage for booze or drugs and never return. The homeless shelter and Bean's café in downtown Anchorage were both full of village people.

"We lose people to the city and the life there," Charlie said. Everyone at the table nodded.

If that was not bad enough, young girls that hit the streets in Anchorage often ended as prostitutes. It was a bad deal, to be sure. Chief Snow had heard about one such case, Mary Frank, but there was little he could do from Togiak other than notify the authorities in Anchorage.

Mary Frank was a sixteen-year-old village girl, young and pretty, a high school junior and Alaska Native. She went to Anchorage for normal things people go to the big town for, some medical appointments, dental work, supplies, or to visit family there.

"I want Chief Snow to go to Anchorage and track her down," Charlie said. "I would go myself, but I gotta get my boat to Dillingham, get it ready for fishing."

This was a very unusual proposition and one which Chief Snow was sure would never in a million years be approved. The money it would cost would be the most immediate roadblock. But then a surprise.

"It's approved then. We will authorize Chief Snow to go to Anchorage to work with the authorities there to find Mary Frank," Mayor Moses announced after very little deliberation.

CHAPTER 3
THE FIRE

After the meeting, Chief Snow drove the four-wheeler home—to the Round House. There, he was greeted by Lilly and his sidekick, Stanley Beans. Lilly was in the kitchen, as usual, and Stanley was over doing laundry—and for the company. He was single and often grew lonely. Snow had noticed that Stanley was hanging around even more since Lilly came into the picture.

Snow entered in a huff.

"I can't believe they actually want me to go to Anchorage and look for this girl. I mean I don't have any real authority there. I know Anchorage, so that's a good thing, but I don't really know Mary Frank. I know a few people down there, but not many law enforcement contacts."

Lilly and Stanley just listened.

"Gee, plane ticket and hotel costs. It's going to cost a fortune," Snow continued.

"Well, if you're going, I am going too," Lilly said like it was already fact.

"What? Gee, Lilly, I don't think so. I mean, I would love for you to go with so you could shop and stuff . . . but the money. I mean we can't really afford that right now. And I will be working."

Lilly's hands were on her hips, and she had turned around approximately at the word *shop* and faced Snow. Her beautifully shaped face was suddenly set with a fierce, determined look.

"I am going with to Anchorage, me and Stanley both," Lilly said, agitated Snow treated her like she was helpless. *It's how men are,* she thought. *They always must be in charge and saving or protecting the women. As if women only wanted to shop.*

"I know Mary Frank; she's my cousin. And I have a place for us to stay in Spenard," Lilly said.

"Spenard? Yikes, that's kinda rough, ain't it?" Snow said, remarking on the area of Anchorage known for being a rough and tumble part of town.

"Depends on what part," Stanley added. "Some parts of Spenard ain't so bad."

"I am very surprised the council approved me to go. I am certain they are not going to approve of you guys going too," Snow said timidly.

"Annie Blue and Mayor Moses want me to go. It is part of the reason they brought it up. I mean, I told Charlie and them we needed to do something about this and encouraged them to send you to help me find her," Lilly said.

Snow wandered over to the window of the Round House. It was late and getting dark out.

The Round House was an old wood stave water tank that sat on the northern edge of town next to a small office building that had once been part of a salmon cannery in Togiak but was now closed. The house sat close to the beach right behind a five-foot seawall.

The water tank had been converted into a living facility thirty years ago by the looks of things. The main living area was on the second floor up a metal spiral staircase in the middle. The main room where they were all at was round except for a small bedroom that interrupted the arc of the circle on one side. The living room area had several large windows facing the river and the bay. Snow spent a lot of time taking in the view. At this moment, he thought he could see the lights of a boat out by the point. It was unusual to see lights out on the water this time of year. *Wonder if it's Charlie,* he thought.

Snow replayed the council meeting in his mind, wondering if the discussion about finding the girl had been inspired by Lilly. Suddenly, having a girlfriend was getting more complicated. He turned and wandered back to the center of the room, where Stanley and Lilly had been chatting about Anchorage.

"Lilly, I wish you had talked with me first, so I knew what was going on," Snow said as diplomatically as he could.

"Eeee. It just came up when I ran into the mayor and Annie at the clinic. I thought you would be happy. I want you to find Mary, Brady!" Lilly pleaded. "That's all."

Stanley's ears perked up. There it is again, that name. *Brady.*

"Eeee, Brady, we thought you'd be happy," Stanley said. He was kind of testing the waters of familiarity.

Chief Snow ignored Stanley and went over to Lilly. He embraced her and held it for a minute.

After the hug, he said, "What we have here is a failure to communicate." A favorite line from an old movie. Was it an old Paul Newman movie?

"I think, sometimes, I can be difficult," Snow said in her ear.

"Sometimes?" she whispered back.

"I am not used to being someone's boyfriend." He was feeling a bit down at this point. His latent loneliness was bubbling up. He did not want to in any way screw up his relationship.

"Me too," she said. They both smiled at her subtle joke.

Snow looked over to where Stanley was standing. He had the

decency to be looking out the windows at the bay while Snow and Lilly were in close to each other.

"Deputy Beans?" Chief Snow said. "Lilly calls me Brady cause she's my girlfriend. I am pretty sure you are not my girlfriend. Please call me Chief Snow, or just Chief. Got it?"

"Eeee, Chief," Stanley said, both smiling.

The three of them began to plan for the trip to the city.

"How much of the Filipino language do you speak?" Snow asked Lilly.

"I am pretty fluent in Ilocano, less so in Tagalog. Some Spanish, too, and Yupik, of course," Lilly said.

"Gee, you must be pretty smart. I can hardly handle English, though I can speak some of the local language," Snow said.

"So, how well do you know this girl who is missing, Mary Frank?"

"Not very well, really. I only met her a couple times. She is my cousin, but we were not close. She is younger than me by quite a bit," Lilly explained.

"I know Mary Frank. I think she is a good kid, though she may be a little wild. But she is like dozens of other young village girls, you know? They go to Anchorage and get exploited, mixed up in the wildness, the nightlife. I know we can't save everyone, but we have to try, don't we?" Lilly pleaded.

"I know that!" Snow said forcefully. "But why us? Why us, and why now? You said it yourself, you hardly know Mary Frank," Snow asked Lilly.

"Why not us? If not us, then who?" Lilly shot back. "Yes, it's true, I don't know her that well. But she needs us. We have to care about her. We have to!" Lilly said near tears.

Lilly had seen enough. She had seen enough damage. Working in health care, she knew what happened, what went on. Young girls like Mary Frank get used and abused. By men, bad men. But this time, she had an opportunity. She wanted to do something, to act. Not just say, *Oh, that's the way things are, that is what happens.* This was apparently her time to say *enough.*

"Brady!" Lilly bellowed. "Stop it! Don't you dare back down now. It's not the kind of man you are. You must step up. This is important, a chance to make a difference! A chance to save a young girl!"

What kind of man am I? Chief Snow thought. *I don't know if I can do this thing Lilly asks. Lilly has an inflated view of me. I don't know about this,* thought Snow. *It felt like this was going to be hard to control, and he did not like the feeling. What's the plan?*

"Do you have an idea of what to do when we get there?" Snow asked Lilly.

Lilly looked at Snow and gave him a look like she understood how he was feeling.

"You will think of something!" she said and gave him a hug. Lilly looked up into his face, her face streaked with tears. She mouthed the words *I love you* to Chief Snow.

"Well, fuck it. We are going to Anchorage!" Snow said with a hug.

"Well, there are some homeless camps we can check. I can contact Tom Begich, you know the guy who came out here for the Tribal Court. He might be able to help if he's not in Juneau.

■ ■ ■

Snow first met Tom Begich when he flew to Togiak as state consultant for development of the Togiak Tribal Court. Snow went to the airport to pick up this VIP consultant, a man who has a long history of working with Tribal groups, he had heard. He was waiting for some guy in a suit, or at least clean clothes, to step off the Cessna Caravan. He saw a guy with long hair, wearing a green army jacket and jeans, get off the plane. *Can't be him,* thought Snow. But in fact, it was. *I guess that's what a VIP looks like in Alaska,* thought Snow. He had a woman in tow that looked more the part. In fact, she was Alaska's attorney general. She had the lost look and clean clothing of a newcomer to the village. She had come along with Tom to see the court.

"Let me help you with that," said Snow, and he tossed their bags in the back of the pickup for the ride into town. He handled the luggage with the rough indifference of someone used to tossing bags.

"I am not letting you handle my guitar!" Tom said with a smirk, his eyes glancing over at the bags in the bed of the truck.

"Oh, hey, sorry. Guess I was a little rough on your things," Snow remarked.

"Kind of how it goes. The pilots often just throw the bags out onto the strip. Better to have some tough baggage or a seabag out here," Tom said.

"Sounds like you've been in the bush before?" Snow said.

"Oh, yeah. Everywhere from Point Hope to Angoon, and most villages around the state."

"Wow, that's impressive. I mean, really, that is a lot of villages to travel to. All for work?"

"Mostly. I mean, I have been to some villages, when I was a kid with my dad, campaigning. I went to many villages for Tribal Courts, but yours is by far the most successful so far. It's kind of a new-old idea. Legal issues usually end up wrapped around the axle. But the Togiak Court is humming right along. I came here to see what you are doing, what's going right, and I heard you are the guy I need to talk to," Tom said.

"No, not really. I mean, Mayor Moses or one of the Elder Judges would be the folks to chat with," Snow said.

"Yeah, I get that, and of course, I will. But you are the one who seems to be driving this forward, where others have gotten jammed up," said Begich as Snow was driving into town. The AG was sitting quietly, listening, and watching out the window as they drove. Snow admired the fact that she was not chattering away trying to impress. The view was mostly a white landscape as far as the eye could see.

Snow shot Tom a quick look and kind of motioned with his eyes at the AG. He made a look that he hoped conveyed his thoughts of *Is she okay?*

They shared a look and smiled.

That evening, Snow escorted the two dignitaries to the Elder Court where he prevailed as a sergeant of arms of sorts.

"All rise!" Snow announced.

The Elders came in from the side door off and walked to their chairs and table on the stage of the big main room of the hall.

There were several people in the room, including the AG and Tom Begich.

Chief Snow was at a table facing the judges. He had papers in front of him relating to the cases. This was not how he had planned things. He had hoped for a case involving a younger child. But instead, the case in front of the Elders that day was that of a sixteen-year-old who had violated curfew and was drinking alcohol. Minor consuming. This was exactly the type of case Snow did not wish for.

The young man in question had already had scrapes with the police. He was not the kind of young person that would normally be receptive to Tribal Court. But the Elders wanted the case, so Snow brought it forward despite his doubts.

Snow announced the case. A sullen looking teenage boy came forward and plopped into a chair, reclining back in the chair, almost lying down. His hat was on backwards, and his entire demeanor announced his lack of respect for the proceeding.

Snow got a bit emotional as he remembered what happened.

Kenny Toovak was the chief judge that day. He was a large man, clean shaven with a buzz haircut. He had a large face and jowls. Snow thought he resembled a walrus, and he was reminded of Lilly's grandfather. He had on an impressive parky of various colors and a wolf ruff. The coat was unzipped.

He slowly stood and limped down the steps one at a time to get down off the stage. The room was quiet, no one knowing what to expect. Judge Toovak majestically limped over to stand directly in front of the youth.

"Sit up. Take your hat off! Show some respect," Elder Toovak said in a quiet voice that everyone could hear.

The young man sat up a bit straighter, but not all the way, as if to say he'd play along, doing his best to look unimpressed.

"I knew your father. He was a captain of a whaling crew. Your family's crew," Toovak began. He was talking in a low voice directly to the youth.

"Your father came from a line of whalers. He was a noble man, a good man. He led the crews to catch whales for food, not just for his clan, but for the village. I admired your father, and his father before him. This is your legacy. This is your heritage." Toovak spoke in a deliberate, singsong fashion, the manner of speaking English in the village.

As he spoke, the young man slowly came to attention. Then he became emotional and began to sob as the Elder talked about his father dying in a whaling accident. It had been tragic, but whaling was dangerous business.

The Elder came forward and placed his hand on the young man's shoulders. The other judges had magically descended and were now gathered around the young man.

"You are the future of your clan. It is a burden to lose your father. It is a burden to lead your clan, to captain a whaling crew. But it is a noble burden. We need you to carry that burden. We will help you carry it, to learn the ways," Elder Toovak said.

The young man was sobbing harder now, hat taken off and in his hands. All the judges placed hands on him.

As it turned out, the power and magic of the court had been put on display for the people who had traveled to see it in action. Everyone in the room had been moved to tears. The young man had been touched by the court and support from his Elders. Snow had been once again surprised at the wisdom of the Elders. The crimes the teen had committed were a product of the young man being lost because his father had died. The Elders knew this, looking to take steps to repair what was damaged in the young man.

■ ■ ■

Snow was recalling that day with the AG and Tom Begich as he looked out the windows of the Round House. It made him emotional reminiscing about it. It was dark out now, so there was nothing much to see, but he was lost in thought and peered out at the blackness. After a minute, he noticed what appeared to be a fire flickering on the beach, upriver from the Round House. *Who would have a fire on the beach at night in this weather,* thought Snow? It was cold, snowing a bit, the wind blowing. It was highly unusual.

"I'm going to check on something, Lilly!" Snow hollered.

"I'm right here. You're hurting my ears!" she replied. Lilly had quietly joined Snow in looking out the window, but he had not noticed her sidle up behind him. She was like that; she often moved silently like a spirit. Snow jumped, startled.

"How do you do that?! You scared the poop out of me!" Snow said. He felt funny saying *poop* but was trying not to swear so much at Lilly's urging.

"You mean *shit*?" she asked, and they both smiled. It sounded like a child swearing when Lilly said a bad word. She did it just to make him smile, and it worked.

"What you doing?" she asked.

Snow told her about the fire, and she looked out at the beach.

"I don't see anything. Just go smoke then!" she said, guessing Snow was just looking for an excuse to have a cigarette. Lilly disapproved of Snow's smoking habit, and he was trying to do it less now that she was in his life. It was a hard habit to break and seemed to be a big part of village life.

"Back in a few," he said as he grabbed his coat.

And smokes.

Chief Snow putted up the beach toward the fire he had seen. Snow headed upriver, away from the Togiak Bay, and toward Walrus Islands. He saw the fire sputtering in the wind up ahead. It looked like two people were around the fire. He approached slowly and stopped down from the fire which was nestled under the lee of the cut bank carved by high tides. He dismounted and approached the fire.

"Coming in!" he announced in the time-honored fashion so as not to surprise anyone and accidently get shot.

"Aye, we heard yee coming a while ago. Pull up a chair!"

He sat on a log close to the fire, hoping that he would be up wind from the smoke. He was, but the wind was swirling. It felt good by the fire.

It was dark and cold. Near to the fire, Snow's eyes adjusted to the light. Because of that effect, he could not see much beyond— only darkness.

"Kinka! What in the hell are you doing out here?" Snow exclaimed with genuine pleasure.

Kinka was of the mysterious, mythical Little People, known locally as the Enukin. He sat with his back to the cut bank, hands and feet stretched toward the fire.

Kinka looked the same as Snow remembered. He was maybe four feet tall, at most, and fine boned. He had a long thin face and nose to match. His outstretched hands had remarkably long fingers. His skin was dark brown as were his eyes, which sparkled in the firelight. He wore what appeared to be fine hand-sewn clothing, including a hat, made from hides, and fur, the kind of clothing you would see in a museum of Native American attire. Surprisingly, he spoke with a kind of English accent. He had a homemade pipe in one of his outstretched hands. On his feet, he wore a fine pair of mukluks.

Chief Snow had heard of the Little People but thought it was just some hokey legend. That changed one night when he was flying back from Dillingham and the plane had fuel problems and set down, crashing on a frozen lake. Unhurt, the passengers began to hike to a hunting cabin when they were attacked by a bear. Snow was mauled by the bear as the other passengers fled for their lives. He had been able to get his sidearm out and put some shots into the bear before it likely would have killed him. He had lost consciousness and a lot of blood. When he came to, he was injured and alone in the dark and cold. He would likely have died from exposure, but Kinka came along and led him to an ancient unknown cabin.

Kinka treated his bear wounds with some herbs and fed him some caribou stew. At the time, Snow thought it may have been a dream or delusion. But the doctor who later treated his wounds noted that they looked remarkably clean and free of infection. He kept quiet about his experience with Kinka until he met Lilly's Oppa, her grandfather, Niki Wassillie. For some reason, he felt comfortable sharing his experience with Oppa Niki. Nikki confirmed that he had heard about Kinka the Kind of the Little People, and other stories of Little People from other members of his clan. He was thankful he talked to Niki, for it made him feel less crazy.

"About time you got here, Snow. I did not know if yee would make it," Kinka remarked, the two sitting by the fire.

"What the hell are you two doing out here?" said Snow.

"Waiting for yee," said Kinka.

Snow looked over at Charlie Johnson, the other person sitting by the fire. Charlie had not spoken but was staring at Snow. Something was not right with Charlie; he looked a bit off. In fact, he looked like he was not all there.

"You okay, Charlie? Thought you were taking the boat to Dillingham," Snow said after a minute. He was aware of Charlie staring at him and was a bit uncomfortable with that fact. Charlie had that effect on people.

The three of them had their fates inexplicably intertwined somehow. Kinka had appeared to Charlie that time and told him to go upriver.

"I didn't make it to Dillingham. My boat went down," Charlie said.

"How'd you make it?" Snow asked.

"I didn't," Charlie said.

Snow looked first at Kinka, then he turned and looked harder at Charlie who was staring off in the distance.

As he looked at Charlie, the smoke and embers obscured him. But it seemed like the smoke and sparks were not going in front or around him, but they were going through him. Charlie seemed to shimmer or flicker, like an image on a computer screen. He looked back at Snow and seemed to wink out for a second.

"My boat got sideways and took a wave over the starboard bow. It was rough out there, but I always liked it rough. I fought it, but I took another wave over the side and the boat rolled. I couldn't make it out," Charlie said somberly and with finality.

Snow didn't know what to say, but finally was able to get some words out that he had been holding onto for some time.

"Thank you for saving my life that day, Charlie. Buck was gonna kill me for sure if you hadn't come along. Thanks to you, and to Kinka the Kind. And Charlie, I am proud to call you my brother," Snow said as his voice cracked.

Charlie looked at Snow and flashed his big wolfish smile.

"You need to find your mother, Snow. She is in Sitka and goes by the name Lanny Brady. Find her and settle your account," Charlie said.

"My mother?" Snow said.

Snow was adopted and had never known his birth mother. He had not sought her out, though he had often wondered about his mom.

"Yes, find your real mother and find out who you really are," Charlie said, looking at Snow.

He appeared to be fading, like he was transparent. Snow could see through him and see smoke on the other side. Then he shimmered a bit and was gone. Snow turned to Kinka.

"Is he gone?" Snow asked.

"Aye."

They sat there in silence for some time.

Chief Snow felt out of it. The whole experience had left him off balance, like the world was shifting under his feet.

"Charlie's right, you know. You should go find your mother, Lanny, and have a nice chat," Kinka said.

"Lanny?" Snow said.

"Yes. Lanny Brady in Sitka, she is your real mom. You need to find her," Kinka said.

"Thank you for letting me talk to Charlie before he left," Snow said with a catch in his voice. "Why do you always help me out, Kinka?"

Kinka got up, leaped high in the air, and landed on Snow's shoulders, then lit back on the ground. It happened in an instant. It was not possible, but it happened, nonetheless. When Kinka landed on his shoulders, it felt like someone just tapped him, very lightly. Snow never moved.

"Why?" Kinka asked with a cackling laugh, almost like a giggle.

"There is no *why*. There simply *is*," Kinka said cryptically. Kinka leapt over the fire and kicked up some sparks and smoke as Snow covered his eyes. Then Kinka was gone, too.

Snow didn't want to hang around out there by himself. He was a bit spooked by it all. He kicked sand in the fire, started his four-wheeler, climbed on, and lit a smoke. Then putted slowly back to the Round House. Once there, he trudged slowly up the spiral staircase to the second floor where he and Lilly lived.

"I thought you were going up the beach. Change your mind?" Lilly asked.

"What? I've been gone for half an hour," Snow responded.

"Silly, you just left. I thought maybe you forgot something; you were only gone a minute," Lilly said.

Snow was not sure of anything at this point. He sat with her on the green and red sofa and explained what had just occurred. Lilly listened raptly without interruption.

"You think I'm crazy?" he asked Lilly.

When he was done talking, he lay down and put his head in her lap. She put her hand on his forehead and straightened his hair.

"I think I love you," she said. "But yes, you are crazy!" she teased.

"I think you should find your mom," she said, agreeing with the advice from Kinka and Charlie.

The phone rang. It was loud, a 1980's vintage tan Ma Bell phone made to withstand a nuclear bomb. It had the old-style bell inside, and Snow had turned it up all the way to make sure it would wake him when it rang in the middle of the night.

Snow leapt up to try and grab it on the first ring.

He got it just in time and put it to his ear. He walked around a bit, having installed a fifty-foot cord so he could walk around, literally, the house, holding the phone with one hand and the base with the other.

He listened for a bit, said a couple things, then hung up.

"Charlie?" Lilly asked.

"Eeee. The ELT went off on his boat. The Coasties called, said they will launch at first light to search for Charlie and his boat."

■ ■ ■

The morning after the fireside chat with Kinka and Charlie was busy. Although Snow assumed Charlie was dead and gone, he still needed to coordinate the search and rescue, or SAR, which was now a search and recovery.

The U.S. Coast Guard had a major air station in Kodiak. They launched one of their orange and white rescue helicopters shortly after dawn. They ran along the beach looking for signs of a boat down or a body washed up ashore. The crew on board included a couple rescue swimmers in case they had to lower someone down to the water.

At about the same time, a couple boats left from Togiak. People were good about helping in a SAR situation. You never knew when you might be the one who needed the help. They had a diver with them just in case. The boats left Togiak in the general direction of the Walrus Islands. They would shortly begin to head easterly toward the point.

"I got a bad feeling," Stanley Beans said to Snow.

For good reason, thought Snow. *Stanley's intuitive.*

They were in the police shack alone now. Getting some coffee and making a game plan, Snow had spread out a couple good nautical maps on the desk by the door, the one Stanley usually sat at.

"Why's that, Stanley?" Snow asked.

"Charlie is the best skipper I ever saw. But he liked to take risks, too. I just think he might not have made it this time," Stanley said.

"Never know, coulda had problems and had to beach the boat. He could be on the beach waiting for someone to pick him up," said Snow, trying to sound optimistic.

"Eeee," Stanley said. "But I don't think so."

The Coast Guard chopper located Charlie's boat quickly. It had rolled over after it had gone down. It was in the area of Anchor Point, the first major point southeast of Togiak. It made some sense as there was deep water there, making the conditions more dangerous. Also, there were reports of shallows or sandbars near the point. Charlie must have been in close to the point, because his boat was found in shallow water heeled over to one side. There was debris floating around the wooden boat, which appeared to be breaking up.

Snow was monitoring the radio and heard the Coast Guard chopper pilot give coordinates to the boats in the water, so they could come directly to the site. Snow marked the spot on the map he had laid out. The Coast Guard chopper lowered a swimmer down, but the swimmer could not safely get into the boat. They flew up and down the coast for a while looking for Charlie as the boats made their way to their location. There was still some hope that he was on a beach somewhere.

The boats from Togiak made it to the wreckage and a diver went in the water. He came up after a minute and said Charlie was in the cabin, apparently drowned. He went back down and was able to finagle Charlie's body out of the cabin and to the surface. Meanwhile, the chopper had come back and was lowering a swimmer down in a basket that looked kind of like a wire cot.

The Coast Guard swimmer and the local diver maneuvered Charlie's body into the basket and reeled him up, then the Coast Guard lowered the basket and retrieved the swimmer. The chopper announced they were enroute to Dillingham to offload Charlie's body. There was no medical examiner in Dillingham to perform an autopsy, but sometimes, in cases that seemed straight forward, they would simply have a physician do an examination.

The whole operation out on the water took several hours, which was pretty quick for a SAR. Charlie, Chief Snow's half-brother, was gone.

CHAPTER 4
THE GIRL

Mary Frank was sixteen going on seventeen and a high school junior. The school she attended was for all grades, as was the case in most small villages. As such, the school functioned as a community center. The gym was open most nights; a place kids could go shoot hoops for a few hours. And community gatherings were often held there. Sometimes they would haul a bunch of whale meat into the gym and the community would gather and process it, an important cultural function.

Mary was born out of wedlock. Her mother had been drinking and partying a lot back then and had been sexually assaulted more than once at drunken house parties. The mother did not know who the baby's father was. Mary's mom talked to her parents, and they all agreed she would keep the baby and the grandparents would help raise her. This was all too common in the village.

Mary felt like she was going crazy and wanted to escape the suffocating, dead end life in a small village. She had matured earlier than many of her classmates, so she felt like she had little in common with them. The boys in particular seemed so immature, and her studies bored her. She had little direction and, consequently, little hope.

In Mary Frank's mind, the village was dirty and boring. Nothing ever happened there. She longed to see something new, something exciting. She thought a lot about Anchorage. She had been there before when she was younger and dreamed of visiting again—maybe even living there. She remembered the malls and stores and the restaurants. Things seemed so shiny and clean. It seemed more exciting to her than Togiak, and though she was a bit frightened by the big city, she was also drawn to it.

Mary Frank's short life had not been an easy one. She resented her mother for foisting off parental responsibilities onto Mary Frank's grandparents. While she saw her mother on an almost daily basis, they had very little mother-daughter interactions. Her grandparents seemed so old and out of touch, which made relating to them difficult.

When Mary Frank was thirteen, her grandfather took an interest in her sexually. She did not know what was going on, only that suddenly he treated her differently. She noticed him staring at her, especially when she was wearing tight clothing. He wanted her to come sit with him and would touch her in ways that made her feel uncomfortable. She knew her grandfather loved her, but this felt funny. Wrong. Then it happened.

She was in her bed one night when her grandfather came in and sat next to her. He did not say anything, and she could smell alcohol on him. He started to rub her back and then probed with his hands until he touched her breast. She felt some excitement but also revulsion. She pulled away from him but was too frightened to say anything. He said some soothing words and left her that night. But he would return, and he got more insistent.

Mary Frank talked to her grandmother. Instead of giving any

details, she simply told her that Grandpa was coming into her room at night. And she did not like it; she didn't want him to come in there anymore. She did not say anything about him touching her ass; she felt shame. It was clear that her grandmother did not understand her, or at least she was not going to do anything about it. Mary would have to deal with it on her own.

One night, her grandfather was drinking and came into her room and again began to touch her. She was young and afraid. She let him touch her breasts and then he touched her crotch and was rubbing it. It felt good but at the same time felt wrong and frightening. It was dark in the room, but she could tell her grandpa was breathing heavier. He pulled the blanket aside and climbed on top of her. She lay there in terror while he thrust his hips at her. She could feel his erection. He was grabbing her breast while he humped on the outside of her panties. She squirmed a bit, but he was heavy and surprisingly strong. He was done quickly and left without a word. It changed her.

Mary Frank tried to talk to her mother about what was going on, but she simply did not want to hear about it. "Lock your door! Stop wearing skimpy clothing around the house," was about all her mother would say. It made Mary Frank feel like, somehow, the groping was her fault. She felt alone and isolated.

Mary Frank took matters into her own hands, to a degree. She got a small hook lock for her room to keep her grandpa from coming into it. She also got in the habit of going out when her grandpa was drinking. She would go find someplace to hang out, and sometimes would simply drive around on her four-wheeler. One such night, Chief Snow waved at her, and they stopped and chatted.

"Hey, whatcha doing?" Chief Snow asked Mary. It was late and well past curfew.

For some reason, she felt okay talking to him. It seemed like he was actually talking *to* her and not just *at* her. She liked that.

"Not doing nothing, really, just driving around," Mary replied.

"Yeah, kinda boring around here, I suppose," Snow said. "But it's getting late. You should probably be home in bed. School tomorrow." Snow sensed something else was going on. "Can't you go home? Something going on?"

Mary Frank was not sure how much to say. She did not want to get her grandfather in trouble, because she instinctively felt it would come back down on her. And she also felt shame.

"They are drinking at my house, and I don't want to be around it," she finally said.

Snow looked at her. She was too young to be out at this time of night. But he understood that this young girl probably felt unsafe. He also did not want to betray her confidence by suddenly making this a police matter.

"Sometimes people do things when they are drinking that they would not normally do. I know how it goes. You don't want to be around it, and that's good. That is understandable and it's okay." He stared at her, weary. "But you also can't stay out all night. I will be out and about tonight. If you are frightened to go home, I can take you there and make sure you are safe. Unless there is someplace else you can go," Snow said.

"I'm okay. I just needed to get out of there for a while. I can go home soon, I think."

Chief Snow looked at her for a minute, thinking. "Okay, thirty minutes, then home. I will be out, so I will know if you go home or not. Okay? And if you need any help, you know you can talk to me, right?"

Mary smiled at Chief Snow and agreed. He seemed nice. More importantly, he did not seem to judge her or preach at her.

■ ■ ■

Mary Frank continued to live in fear of her grandfather, but as she matured, he and other men increasingly ogled her. By age fifteen, Mary matured into a full-figured beauty, attracting increasing attention from both high school boys and men.

One of her mom's male friends invited her to a party one night. This was not that unusual in the village. It seemed innocent enough at the time. And she felt cool that a grown man invited her to a party. So, she went.

It seemed fun and so adult. It was mostly men drinking. The man who invited her asked her if she wanted to try a drink of alcohol. She agreed and took a sip. It tasted terrible, burning her mouth and throat, but then she got a warm feeling in her stomach and felt good. And the men in the party were so attentive and flattering toward her. She felt popular and appreciated.

Mary Frank began going to parties with her new adult friends. She got very drunk one night and ended up having sex with the man who had invited her. She did not even remember it that well. She was so drunk that night; she could hardly walk.

■ ■ ■

The next few days and weeks, she was very worried that maybe she had gotten pregnant. She went to the village medical clinic and met with her cousin Lilly Wassillie who was working as a health aide.

"Are you having sex now?" Lilly asked her bluntly.

"Only once, I mean I am not like out doing it all the time," Mary Frank stammered.

"You need to protect yourself, Mary. You don't want to accidentally get pregnant. Have you talked to your mom or anybody else about birth control, things like that?" Lilly asked.

They talked some more, but it was clear to Lilly that Mary did not have an adult around to mentor her. Mary did not open up completely to Lilly, as she was still feeling too ashamed and isolated. There was no way she was going to talk about what her grandpa had done to her. She liked Lilly, though, and took some comfort from the visit.

She soon was drawn back to the party life and began to smoke marijuana often. Mary had smoked pot with kids her age a couple times. But this was different. She was now partying with adults.

Smoking pot made her feel calm, and that life was not so bad, after all. She could laugh at things when she was high. She also liked smoking pot because she felt more in control than when she drank alcohol, that she could more easily avoid the frequent sexual advances of the men at the parties. It was only when she got drunk that she found it more difficult to fend men off. Still, on occasion, she would get drunk, which led to, again, having sex with men much older.

At one of the parties, Mary Frank had a conversation with Nancy Pook. Nancy and her husband, James, attended most parties in the village and were known to get wild, especially James. Even so, Mary took a liking to Nancy who seemed to be generally interested in her.

The two ended up talking about Anchorage and the life there.

"If I were young and pretty like you, that's where I'd be headed," Nancy had said. "Lots of opportunity there for a pretty thing like you."

The seed was planted.

CHAPTER 5
SITKA SNOW

Chief Snow decided to follow up on the lead he was given about his mother and flew to Sitka. He knocked on the door of a large, framed house that appeared to be very old and in disrepair like so many buildings in the old part of Sitka near the water. The house was just a couple blocks from the Alaska Public Safety Academy where Snow was staying.

Among Sitka's claims to fame is that it was where the transfer of ownership ceremony occurred in 1867. The United States paid Russia $7.2 million for the land that is now Alaska, just two cents per acre.

Sitka had been the state's capital until Juneau stole the crown in the early 1900s. Sitka became a city borough of the new state capital, the largest city borough in terms of landmass in the US. It is comprised of just 8,800 residents but occupies around 4,800 square miles.

It was along the streets of an old, somewhat dilapidated neighborhood that Snow came face-to-face with his birth mother,

Lanny Brady. He found her address, knocking on the door of her ramshackle house, unannounced.

It had been easy to locate his mother, Lanny Brady. He got her name, and that she was in Sitka, from Kinka. He did some research and found that she was working at the local Tribal Agency. With some trepidation, he reached out to her via email. She had responded, and they had planned on meeting. That time had come.

When the door opened, Lanny Brady and Chief Snow were face to face. It was a moment neither would forget. They looked at each other for a few intense moments. Lanny looked shocked to see him standing there, even though she was expecting him. Her eyes were large as she looked him up and down. Snow was reserved, not knowing what to say or how to react. Lanny finally moved forward and pulled him into an embrace.

Neither Lanny nor Chief Snow was fully prepared for this moment, the emotional sledgehammer of meeting. Lanny was numb but started moving.

Lanny invited her son in and led him to a small room, perhaps an old bedroom or something that had been converted into an office or study. The space was small and filled with various Tribal artworks and other items.

Lanny took her seat and Snow sat across from her. He looked around the room. There were several candles burning at various points around the room, one on the coffee table, one on an end table, and many several other places. There was a single electric light from a small dim lamp on the end table next to Lanny.

There was a bookshelf against one wall. Several appeared to be Tribal, historical books. He saw titles about Tlingit and Haida Native Alaskans. One book on the coffee table was titled *Customs of the Tlingit Indians of Alaska* and had a photo of a Native man in full regalia.

He took stock of the other items in the room. A red and black blanket with a Tribal design was hanging on the wall. Next to the blanket hung a spruce root hat on a nail. He saw several masks arrayed on the walls around Lanny. The masks appeared to be made either from baleen or a similar material. One appeared to be carved from some type of bone.

He also saw several baskets of various sizes in the room. One was quite large and looked to be made of reeds. There was a smaller weaved basket that appeared to be made of a darker material. On the bookshelf was a hand carved bentwood box with a distinctive Tlingit design in the wood and painted in red and black. It looked to be very finely made. On the coffee table was another small box; this one appeared to be made from baleen and had an ivory carved handle on the lid.

The room appeared to be almost like a shrine. There was some type of incense burning on the cluttered coffee table. The smell was not unpleasant. Off to the left of where Snow was sitting, there was an open doorway that led to another room. The doorway was simply black, shedding no light.

"Let me look at you," Lanny said and stood. She indicated with her hands that Snow should stand, and he did. Tears welled in her dark eyes. She was probably in her late forties. She had on a Tribal robe of red and black, with many buttons. Her straight black hair hung almost to her waist. She had an easy but nervous smile which just seemed to magically appear at any moment. Even though her eyes were damp, she appeared happy.

Lanny took his face in her hands. She was several inches shorter than Snow, so she was peering up into his face, showing her straight white teeth.

"In my mind, you are still a baby or a child. I thought about you a million times, but I could never envision what you may look like as an adult. So, you remained a child in my mind," she said, tilting her head as she changed perspectives.

"I have to tell you that I always wondered about my heritage; I thought I was white for the longest time," Snow said. "But—"

Lanny gave him a warm embrace, and then returned to the worn, brown, leather, easy chair she had been sitting in.

"But what?" she asked.

"I began to wonder if I may be part Native. I knew I was adopted but was never curious about my heritage until recently," Snow said. "I mean, well, I guess I always thought I may be of mixed blood, but it just did not seem to be something I was worried about, or even that curious about," Snow said, looking away for a moment.

"What changed?" Lanny asked.

"Shoot. You wouldn't believe me if I told you," he responded.

"I might surprise you," she said.

"I have to say this, and please don't take it the wrong way. I found a kind of comfort in *not* knowing for the longest time. It seemed like it gave me a clean slate, like people could not be put into one box or another. But it started to gnaw at me a bit, not knowing. Then I met—" His thought hung there as he debated whether he should tell her how he found out about her. The whole Little People thing was something he had kept secret from almost everyone.

"I regretted giving you up, Brady. It was something that haunted me for years," she said huskily. She averted her eyes. "I was drinking then. I was young, in Anchorage, going to school, which was good at first, but I got caught up in the party scene and drinking.

"One night, I was at the bar on 4th Avenue in Anchorage, partying with my girlfriends. We were at a bar called the Monkey Wharf. I remember they had little live monkeys in the bar behind a glass wall. I loved to watch the monkeys, and they were watching us," she said.

"I was pretty high, and my friends had all left. I went outside with three men. They invited me to go to a party with them. We were all pretty high," she said. Her words dripped out slowly as if voicing them was painful. She seemed to choke.

"They were white men. They raped me," she said after some time had passed.

"One of those men is your father, but I don't even know who they were," she said with a sob.

"At the time, I just kind of tried to block it out, that it happened. I blamed myself a hundred different ways. I shouldn't have drunk so much, should have left with my girlfriends, on and on," she continued.

"But, mostly, I just tried not to think about it, like it was bad dream," she said. "But then, I became pregnant."

After a minute or so, she continued.

"I didn't think I could raise a baby. And I was so ashamed. Devastated, really," she said. "I had to give you up, Brady. I am sorry."

Lanny talked about her struggles with alcohol and how it took her a long time to overcome, with many setbacks. She got back around to her time in Anchorage and even described how Snow got his name.

"The night I was raped by those men, I remember lying on the ground. I was looking at the snow coming down and it seemed so pure and beautiful. It stuck with me, and I decided to name you Brady Snow. Brady for your family name, and Snow for the one sense of purity, of something good and beautiful, that I took from that awful experience," she explained.

"I don't even know who your father is," she repeated.

"I know who my father is," Snow stated bluntly.

■ ■ ■

In the dark doorway, a shape had materialized as they had been talking. Snow had not seen it at first. But he glanced that way for a moment and saw a woman, what appeared to be a woman, in the blackness of the doorway.

Snow glanced at the doorway and back to Lanny, as if to point out that someone else was nearby.

"That is Kee," she said. "She is my . . . ah, friend," Lanny said with some hesitancy. But then she continued as if she had come to a decision to share some information.

"Kee is a shaman," Lanny said.

"I met a shaman before in the village," Snow said, as if to indicate that it was not anything taboo for him, and that he was not put off by her presence.

Kee stepped out from the shadow of the door a bit. She had on traditional Native clothing. She appeared to be in her early thirties at most. Her hair draped past her waist. But it was not pretty and straight like Lanny's. Instead, it looked snarled and matted. She looked dirty and kind of unkempt; even her face appeared to have grime on it. She had what looked like a rattle in one hand. It was hard to be sure of anything, as she was standing in partial darkness.

Kee spoke in Tlingit to Lanny for some time. Afterward, she retreated to the dark doorway and seemed to wait.

"Kee said she wants to hear your story. I am not sure what prompted her to be here tonight. But she contacted me and asked if she could be here when I met you. I am not even sure how she knew that you were coming," Lanny said.

"I imagine she wants to hear about the Little People," Snow remarked.

Kee shook her rattle. Lanny's eyebrows shot up, and Snow smiled.

"How do you know who your father is, Brady? I don't even know that." Lanny asked.

"An Enukin told me," Snow said. Kee shook the rattle twice. *Good timing on the rattle,* Snow thought wryly.

"I met Kinka the Kind of the Little People. He saved me after I was attacked by a bear," Snow said.

"You were attacked by a bear?" Lanny asked, seemingly astounded. "My word, you have some adventures!"

"Well, you ain't heard nothing yet!" Snow said, and then he and Lanny chuckled. Snow now wished Kee would shake the rattle.

"Before I left Togiak to come here, I saw a fire on the beach at night. I went to check it out. At the fire was Kinka and the spirit of a man named Charlie Wassillie, who had just died in a boat crash," Snow said. Lanny's eyebrows shot up again. Kee shook the rattle twice right after he finished his sentence.

"I know how it sounds. Crazy. But it's all true . . . true to me, anyway. To make a long story short, Charlie and Kinka told me I needed to find you. They told me your name and that you lived in Sitka," Snow continued.

"But that does not explain how you know who your father is," Lanny said.

"Well yeah, you're right. One time, I was in a fight to the death with this bad guy, and Charlie saved my bacon that day. He told me then that Kinka told him I needed to be saved, so he did. But to answer your question about my father, Charlie said Kinka told him he and I were half-brothers. For some reason, this made sense to me, even though Charlie and I were adversaries, with him bootlegging and stuff, and me being a 5-0," Chief Snow said using one of the popular slang terms for the police in Alaska, especially in the bush.

"But at the same time, in my gut, I thought it was true. It's hard to say why, but there was always this connection between Charlie and me. Kind of a wary mutual respect, but somehow *more* than that, *deeper* than that. So, when he told me that we had the same father, it seemed to make sense to me. Charlie's father is a guy from South Naknek named Cliff Johnson. So, my birth father, I believe, is also Cliff Johnson," Chief Snow said.

When Chief Snow spoke the name Cliff Johnson, it sent a jolt through Lanny. The name rolled around in her head. She felt sure she heard that name the night she was raped.

Kee started speaking in Tlingit again, but both Lanny and Snow were not paying her much mind.

"What's she going on about now?" Snow asked Lanny, nodding sideways at Kee.

"Oh, she has questions for you, but before we get to that, I want to know about this Cliff Johnson. Do you know him?" Lanny asked.

"Yes. He runs a bar in South Naknek called The Pit. He also had a well drilling outfit, a store, and some other things going on. I met him plenty of times when I was working up there, before I found out he was possibly my father."

"He does not appear to be a bad man, I don't think. Despite what he did to you. He is certainly ambitious and may be a bit greedy. But he has done some good things, and that tells me he's not all bad. Charlie hated him, but I think that had to do with his father not really claiming him as a son. And Cliff Johnson is white, and Charlie was not fond of white folks generally, or maybe it was simply that he was very proud of his Native side," Snow continued.

"Yes, that would be one of the men who raped me. Since you said the name, it came back to me. The man, Cliff, talked about drilling wells that night," Lanny said. "But how do you *know* he is the one?" How can you be positive?

"Because Kinka and Charlie told me so," the chief said. Kee shook the rattle again, one time. "I mean, I never tracked it down or did a DNA search or anything. It's kinda strange, really. I felt compelled to meet you and find out where I come from. But I never much felt that same interest about Cliff Johnson. I felt like I know what he is about, I guess. But now that I think about it, it would be good to know about my heritage on that side too. Cripes, this is all new to me," Snow said and shook his head.

Kee was speaking Tlingit again to Lanny. Snow interrupted Kee and said, "Do you speak English?"

Kee looked in his direction and finally said, "Yes, of course."

"Then, why don't ya ask me directly what you want to know. It would be a lot easier," Snow said.

Lanny laughed long and loud. Chief Snow smiled at her and raised his eyebrows as if to say, *What?*

"You are definitely my son!" Lanny said and chuckled. "Leave it to my boy to get feisty with a shaman!"

"Okay then," Kee said.

"I want to know what Charlie looked like when you saw him on the beach. Did you see him talk to you? I mean, did you actually see him speak?" Kee asked.

Snow was thinking, *Did I tell her we were on the beach?* He had been around long enough to know that shamans were people, and that meant they had human qualities and failings, just like anyone else. A shaman may have some special power to link with spirits, but they may also be mean or petty or just a good bullshitter.

"I don't remember seeing him actually speak, now that you mention it. I seem to remember knowing what he said. But I did see him smile and saw him laugh," Snow said. "How did you know we were on the beach, and how did you know I was coming here to seek out my mother?"

Kee ignored his questions, instead asking him another, "Have you ever seen a spirit before?"

"You mean besides you?" Snow joked, hoping to lighten the mood. But no one laughed.

"Just kidding. I've never seen a spirit before. But I have seen and talked to Kinka, you know the Enukin, a few times. I am not sure exactly what he is. I mean to say, I don't know if he is a spirit or what. What is Kinka?" Snow asked. *I may as well get something out of this conversation, too,* he thought.

"Did Charlie appear to you or how did you come to see him?" Kee asked.

Chief Snow patiently explained how things happened on the beach. He told her what he remembered, in detail, of that encounter with Charlie's spirit and Kinka.

"And Kinka. What did he look like and how did he act? What did he say?" Kee asked.

"My turn. How did you know I was coming to Sitka to find Lanny? By the way, I can't really see you talk. I can hear your voice, but I can't see your mouth, really. Just the white of your teeth," Snow pressed.

Kee shook her rattle twice. At times, when she shook the rattle, it seemed like it was for emphasis. But Snow was not sure what it meant.

Kee began to chant softly in Tlingit, or that is at least what Snow thought she was speaking. He just knew a couple words. The chanting, dim room, and smokiness from the incense burning made for a gloomy and mysterious atmosphere. Snow had a mild feeling of nausea. He could see her outline in the darkness of the doorway; her form was swaying.

Snow slowly stood, stepping toward Kee in what he hoped was a non-threatening way. Kee did not move back or appear to be put off.

Snow stood a few feet from Kee and looked her over. He wanted to get a measure of this situation, and her. He could see her more clearly, but her features were still kind of soft in the dim glow of the candles nearest to her. She seemed to waiver a bit as the light flickered. Kee was still chanting in a murmur and swaying slightly back and forth. *She may have been attractive once,* Snow thought. She had what seemed like an animal scent—not unpleasant but different than anything he had smelled before. It reminded him of when he smelled the bear as it was mauling him.

"Some have the gift," Kee said to him. "I have the gift, which is how I knew you were coming. But you do not have the gift," she said. "That is why I am asking you questions, to discern what you saw and heard as one who does not have the sight."

"So, what did you figure out then?" Snow asked. He was slightly put off by her statement, but he knew it was true.

"I discovered that you were chosen," she said.

"Great. Chosen for what?" Snow responded.

"I do not know. I only know that you were chosen," she said.

"That could be good, but that could also be bad, really bad."

She shook the rattle hard once, which had the effect of snapping the room and Snow into clarity.

He slowly turned and shuffled back to his chair. He thought for a moment and stood facing the chair with his back to Kee. He had some more questions. He turned and sat and started to ask Kee a question about Kinka but noticed that she no longer appeared to be standing in the doorway.

"She leave?" Snow asked his newly discovered mother, Lanny.

"Eeee. She's gone. It's how she rolls," Lanny said with a brilliant smile. They both chuckled softly.

"Don't say it. I know this was an, um, different experience. But it's better not to talk about it," Lanny said. "I did not plan for this, but it seemed destined to happen."

She focused on her son. "I have a ton of questions about you, and your life. But first, I want to talk to you about your heritage," Lanny said.

CHAPTER 6
LANNY'S STORY

Chief Snow and Lanny had agreed to get together again after their first night. This time, they were alone together. They were seated in the same room as before. Snow looked around and saw that everything looked the same, except that Kee was not standing in the darkened doorway. He saw that his mother, Lanny, had again worn her red and black Tribal robe. She was wearing a spruce root hat that she now took off and set on the crowded coffee table.

The room was dimly lit as before. Lanny lit several candles around the room as Snow patiently watched. She also lit a stick of incense on the coffee table. She moved with practiced patience. As she moved around the room, she had a distinct limp, like her hip was bothering her. There was a solemn quality to her actions.

Before he left last night, they had chatted for some time about his life. Lanny asked him a lot of questions. Her interest piqued as he talked to her about the life in the village, and especially when he talked about the Tribal Court.

"Why did you do that, start a Tribal Court?" she asked him.

"Well, Mayor Moses asked me to," he responded.

"Yes, I see, but you did not know how to do that. You could have simply said you didn't know what to do and begged off." Lanny said.

"We needed to do something; the mayor was right about that, for sure. We were losing too many village kids to drugs and alcohol. The system was simply not working. Mayor Moses said he wanted to try and return to the old ways. I was willing, though if I had known how difficult it was going to be, I may have been less enthusiastic. I mean, it was a real struggle," Snow explained.

Lanny listened attentively.

"Do you think it is working? I mean, the Tribal Court. Do you think it is having an impact on the kids?"

"Yes. At first, I was unsure. The kids were paying attention in Tribal Court, but I needed to see if they were going to re-offend. Also, I was worried that the kids or their parents would not go; it was easy not to go. Tribal Court was more difficult, generally, than the state system. But I was surprised that everyone wanted to go to Tribal Court. Then I was worried about the Elders. Would they be up to the task? None of them have had any training of any kind for this kind of thing," Snow continued.

"So, were your worries justified? How did the Elders do?" she asked.

"My worries were about the local folks, but really the problems were with the state agencies. No one really seemed too crazy about it. Or maybe it was just the normal bureaucracy. I was told to do this and do that, create an MOU, and get it signed, and then the people who told me to get the MOU would not sign it. It sucked," Snow said.

"But then I talked to a trooper friend, Sergeant Dickron. He told me to just go for it, without all the permissions and shit. So, we did."

"Funny thing happened—it worked!" Snow said. "It seemed like everyone locally wanted it to happen, so it was well supported. The kids and parents showed up. The Elder judges always amazed me with their wisdom, and the kids did not re-offend. The main effect, I guess, was that we seemed to stop losing the kids to the system. I mean, they still committed petty crimes, but they did not seem to graduate to the more serious stuff."

"I imagine you were catching them early and setting them on a different path," Lanny commented.

"Exactly. But also, the parents were involved too, and I do not think any of the parents wanted to be back in front of the Elders," Snow said.

"The reason I was asking about the Tribal Court is because I was wondering if somehow you felt your Native roots. I mean, people have been trying to start Tribal Courts in the bush for a while, but it seemed like you got it done. I thought maybe there was something more."

"I just wanted to do something to help. The kids would get in trouble, and nothing would happen. I gave up writing tickets for curfew or other minor offenses because they would never go anywhere. Nothing would happen until a kid would do something serious, and then usually it meant taking them out of the village. Now I can write tickets of minor things and there are consequences.

"Probably the coolest thing is that the kids get to spend time with their Elders. They hear the language; they hear about the old days and their history. And sometimes the work service they have to do is also with the Elders, hauling wood or scooping snow. I suspect there is also some time listening to stories!" Snow said.

"We have a Tribal Court in Sitka. But it's not working too well. It seems like we don't get the referrals; the police department is not really on board," Lanny said with sadness. "We could use your help here, I think."

"Well, it was easy in Togiak because I am the police chief. I did not have to try and convince anyone to do it. And I could intercept the cases that were appropriate for the court and see to it that the kids made it to court. I remember when some folks did not show up to court, I had to take a four-wheeler and go get them," Snow smiled.

Lanny had a lot of questions about Snow and his job in police work. She was also very curious about Lilly Wassillie.

"So, you have a girlfriend, too? You are busy, I think. What is Lillie like?"

Snow took out a picture he had in his wallet. It was already faded and bent in the shape of his butt. But there was no hiding Lillie's beauty.

Lanny held the picture up to the light for some time, really taking a long look.

"She is Yupik, amirite?" she asked.

"Yes. Yupik, Filipino, and a bit white. Mostly Yupik, though," Snow said with some pride.

"I think I can see the Filipino in her. She is beautiful," Lanny remarked, handing the photo back to Snow.

"Do you mind if I smoke?" Lanny asked Snow.

"Oh, gee, you smoke, that's terrible!" Snow said just to see Lanny's face. But before she could respond, he had pulled the pack of Marlboro reds out of his pocket and flashed it.

Lanny smiled, and she led him out to the back porch.

"I was ashamed of smoking, and often have hidden it. One night at my first Tribal Council meeting, they took a break, and most of the council members went out for a smoke . . . me too. I somehow felt more at home after that," Snow said.

"The number of Tribal people who smoke is very high, too high. We have developed prevention and secession programs and the numbers are coming down, though they are still way too high. At least it seems like the younger folks are not picking up the habit," Lanny said.

The two quieted for a bit, taking in what they had discussed. Snow was anxious to learn about his heritage.

First of all, "I am Raven clan of the Kiksadi," Lanny started. "I can't tell you about your father's family history. It sounds like you know more about him than I ever did. But I can tell you about your Native side, your Tlingit family. You actually have a connection to Katlian, who was in the same clan; he was a Raven, too," Lanny said.

Lanny saw a lack of recognition on her son's face. "You know about Katlian," she said.

"Ah, that's a street over by the water, downtown, right?" Snow said.

"Yes. Named after Chief Katlian, your ancestor. I think it is time you heard something about Katlian," she began.

■ ■ ■

Lanny began telling of the folklore about the great chief, her blood relative and Snow's. She spoke, uninterrupted. Snow was mesmerized. It was as if Lanny was there, witness to the events from the early 1800s.

Chief Katlian's heroism was, in fact, a deep part of Alaskan history.

Lanny told of how Chief Katlian was sitting on a log outside the fort.

He was looking at his feet, picking at them. He had some cracking and redness on the bottom of his feet and between the toes. He rubbed some spruce root ointment on them, hoping that would help with the cracking.

His wife, Nami, came up and joined him on the log. Nami took the spruce root ointment from Katlian and rubbed it on his feet for him.

"Maybe you should try Devil's Club instead?" she said.

"I tried that; it worked for a bit, then no more. So now I try spruce root," Katlian responded.

"Wait, are you saying Chief Katlian had athlete's foot?" Chief Snow interrupted Lanny.

"Don't interrupt your mother, especially when she is telling a story!" Lanny shot back, only half joking.

"Does that spruce stuff work? Because I get some rotten feet from time to time," Snow asked.

Lanny ignored him and continued.

"Maybe you should wear those Russian boots you have?" Nami said.

"They are nice, but my feet don't like them," Kat said. "I think I got the rotten foot from the boots."

"Kut, you just need to get used to them," she said.

Her pet name for her husband was Kat, but it sounded like Kut when she said it.

They sat on the log outside the fort built by the Tribe and looked out at the activity around them. It was a sunny day, and calm. It was beautiful in Sheet ka (Sitka) when the sun was shining. Katlian and his wife Nami took some time to simply enjoy the sun. Though it was spring and still cool, the sun had some power to it that day, and warmed their skin. It felt good.

He looked out and saw several canoes nearby going this way and that. He could see the ancient volcano across the bay from where they sat; it was the most distinctive feature of the beautiful landscape around Sitka. The mountain (Mount Edgecumbe) still was covered with snow. It would stay that way until the summer months burned off all the snow.

In front of him was an exposed large gravel spit. This was part of the reason Shaman Stooncook or Stoon had wanted to build the fort in this location; it was not simply the access to the river water. Stoon had explained that the large Russian ships with cannons could not come in close to the fort location because of their deep draft, and the shallows of the gravel flats near the mouth of the river. It made sense, but there were a whole host of other considerations that Katlian and others had raised. At the end of the day, Stoon's position held, and the leaders of the Tribe agreed. And so it was that Katlian was sitting next to the newly completed fort in the location Stoon had suggested.

The fort was sizable. It was called Shishaga Noow and was constructed of green fresh cut timber or saplings. The idea was that the Russian cannon balls would not penetrate the green and springy wood. The fort was large enough for several longhouses inside. The outer structure had been completed, but a number of craftsmen were always making some kind of improvements to strengthen the palisade style walls or working on the clan houses inside the fort. The structure was impressive.

Katlian wore no shirt today, only a breechcloth. Nami was rubbing his back and kept bumping over scars. She glanced at his back. There were multiple scars there from past battles. She examined them more closely for a minute to ensure that everything had healed properly. When satisfied, she turned back to enjoy the view with her husband.

In front of them, they could see Kix working on a canoe. Kix was a cousin to her husband and a trusted confidant. The boat he was working on was a medium size craft that would hold ten warriors or so. The canoe was shaped and hollowed out. He was chipping away with his adze to refine the shape further. Eventually, he would reach the pegs he had placed in small holes drilled through the wood. This was the method developed and passed on to ensure the proper thickness of the hull of the canoe.

Kix was a craftsman at canoe building. It was interesting and hypnotic to watch him work. His canoes were very prized for their overall quality. Some were even adorned with ornamental carvings on the outside of the boat. Katlian did not care about the carvings. He cared about the quality of the canoe. Speed, maneuverability, payload—these were all things Katlian cared about more than the ornamental carvings.

Canoes were the lifeblood of the Tribe. They had used canoes since, well, forever, it seemed. They used canoes to travel to hunting and fishing grounds, to travel to other Tribes for trade, to make war. Canoes were an integral part of Tlingit life.

"I tried to wear the shoes, Nami. I can see the value in them, especially in the winter. And those boots are very nice and protect the feet. But my feet just can't stand being closed in like that," he said.

"Well, I understand, Kut. I prefer to run around naked, you know," Nami said.

Katlian looked over at her to see if she was joking or was serious. But she did not give him a sign as to which it was. He stared at her for a minute and wondered at her beauty.

Nami was a beauty indeed. On that day I speak of, she wore a simple dress made of hides that had been worked to make the hide thin and pliable. She had long hair that she had made into a thick braid that hung down her back like a rope. She had no jewelry or adornments of any kind, though she sometimes had a ring in her nose for special occasions. Some of the Tribal members had tattoos, but she did not prefer to have any.

Nami was about five foot two inches tall, about medium height for Tlingit women. She had heavy bones but was slender, nonetheless. She was small but had the figure of a woman and not a girl. She was strong physically and strong willed. There was a beauty and quiet pride to her appearance. Her face was darker brown that Katlian's. Her beauty seemed to shine out from within.

Katlian knew he had been fortunate to find a wife such as Nami. Not only was she a beauty, but he loved her. And she was smart. Nami was not from his clan, but instead was from the

Eagle clan of the Tlingit Tribe. This had proved very important over time. He was not sure why she chose him. He was feeling the stirring when she spoke and broke the spell.

"I thought Kix had an apprentice working with him? Where did he go?" Nami had asked.

"'His helper is busy today. They are on a trip to the fishing grounds to see if any fish are in yet? It's too early but it's good to check," Katlian said.

"Maybe they are looking for the Kushtaka," Katlian joked. But the Kushtaka was no joke to him.

The Kushtaka was a legend of a creature that was half man, half otter. The stories were many and varied. Sometimes the Kushtaka would do frightening things, like luring hunters to their death, or tricking them. Other times they were helpful, even saving lost hunters. It was an enigmatic legend.

Katlian saw one when he was a young boy of about ten. He had been out in the woods by himself. He made his way back down to the water where he had a tiny canoe. He stopped short of the water when he saw the creature standing in the water. It startled Katlian and he froze in place. The creature looked over at him and they both stared at each other for a bit.

He knew it was a Kushtaka by its appearance. The body was like that of a man, what he could see. But the creatures face was that of an otter. It had a furry head and face, and long whiskers. The eyes were black and deep. It seemed that the Kushtaka had been examining Katlian's canoe. They looked at each other for a time, then Katlian waved his hand. The Kushtaka seemed to smile. Then it turned and went in the water and was gone. He has been waiting to see one again, but it has not happened. Yet.

Katlian stood and stretched, cracking his back and his neck as he did so. He was an impressive man. Very muscular and strong. There was a reason why he had become the Tribe's War Chief. He was a fierce warrior, but also had a tactical mind. He understood strategy of battles and warfare and was good at that aspect as well as the more primal aspects. He was audacious and aggressive and formidable in battle. The Russians had found that out.

"Do you think Stoon is right, that the Russians are coming back, Kut?" Nami asked.

"You don't have to be a Shaman to know that," Katlian said somewhat more sharply than he intended. Nami knew that the sharpness was not directed at her. She understood that her husband, Katlian, was simply not that impressed by the Shaman Stooncook or Stoon.

"I mean, he has an equal chance at being right, and even if the Russians don't come this year, he will make up some kind of excuse to make it seem like he knew it all along," Katlian said bitterly.

"Shush, Kut. You need to keep those feelings hidden. You do not want to make an enemy of Stoon," she said softly.

"He just makes stuff up, sometimes. I mean, maybe he does have the sight, but clearly he speaks out of his ass sometimes," Katlian said more quietly, making a farting noise with his tongue and lips. He looked over at Nami and smiled. She could not help herself, he could always make her laugh, and she giggled now.

"Stop!" she whispered. "You are terrible."

"That's why you love me!" Katlian said and pulled her close.

"Yes, I love you because you can make good farting noises from both ends of your body!'" she whispered and pushed him away playfully.

"Seriously, though. I can tell you the Russians are coming back, and I am no seer. Of course, they are. They left people here at their settlement until we kicked them out. So, yes, the Russians will return; that is a given. I have more issues with Stoon directing the placement of a fort for us to defend. That is serious business. We are placing a lot of faith in Stoon's abilities, and frankly, I am less than convinced of that ability," Katlian said.

This had been a very serious and spirited debate, the Shaman Stoon strongly recommending the move to place a new fort near Indian River. Many of the leaders did not agree, including Katlian. But Stoon was relentless. He said he had a vision that they needed to build a fort that had a good water supply. And the fort needed to be built to withstand the Russian cannons.

"They are coming. You need to listen to me. If not, we may all die by their guns," Stoon had said.

Stoon was a difficult shaman. He had an arrogant manner about him. That arrogance was only part of the reason Katlian did not like Stoon. There was something else about him. Katlian could not put a finger on it, but it was real to him. But Nami was right; it was wise not to go public with those feelings, unless he was ready to make an enemy out of the highly esteemed Shaman.

In the Tlingit culture, the shaman held a position of high regard. They were called upon to cure illnesses, chase away bad spirits, and as a seer, to give advice about future events. The Shaman was their connection to the spirit world and the earth and animals that roamed the surface. They also performed rituals for the Tribe and could even affect the weather. The Tlingit shaman never bathed or washed his hair; that was the custom. In short, a shaman was not someone you wanted to have as an enemy.

"The placement of a fort is something I have knowledge about and some experience. So maybe I am just upset that they would listen to Stoon instead. I will get over it and not do anything to antagonize him," Katlian said to placate Nami.

"Katlian knew Nami worried about things like this. She was his full partner, and he respected her opinion and counsel. More than once, she had given him critical advice that he likely would not have considered. She was more politically astute than he at times; he understood that fact. Also, she could and did float his ideas for battle or other key objectives to her clan members. She *was very subtle in this way. She could help Katlian determine if he would have support from her clan in such things. Her help in this manner was invaluable. Her advice and support were critical in Katlian's rise in the Tribe. That and his hammer!*

"You think the Russians will come this year?" she asked her husband.

"I don't know, but if they are coming this year, I expect them to be coming soon," Katlian replied.

"Going back to work, Kut," Nami said and left him to his thoughts.

Katlian stretched his back out some more. Sometimes he had a crick in his back that he would try to work out. He walked over to talk with Kix, still working on the canoe.

"Kix, how is it coming?" Katlian asked.

It seemed as though Kix had been waiting for someone to come along so he could take a break, because he seemed ready to set down his tools.

"It's good. This is a good tree. That is the first step and can be the most important thing you know," Kix said. "You can make a bad canoe out of a good tree, but you can't make a good canoe out of a bad tree," Kix said.

Katlian took his hand and ran it along the edge of what would later be the starboard side rim of the canoe. He marveled at the amount of planning and time it took to craft a canoe. He did not think he possessed the patience.

"I don't think I have the patience to do what you do, Kix," Katlian said.

"Maybe. But I don't think I can fight like you can either or lead the men in battle. We all have our talents, I guess," Kix said.

"Where is your protégé? Checking on the fish?" Katlian asked.

Kix laughed. "Right! It's fine, he is young and has all his life to work. Today, I think he's out enjoying the fine weather with some other boys. I told them to check on our stores over on the island as long as they are out and about."

"Good. We may have Russians soon, and we will need those stores," Katlian said, referring to the stored gunpowder and extra ammunition they had cached on a small island away from the settlement.

"I supposed they're coming back some time or another. I wish they would just stay in Russia or wherever. We don't need them around here; they are going to be a problem," Kix said.

"Let'em come. They can die here if they do," Katlian said.

■ ■ ■

For the next hour, Lanny continued to tell of the history of Chief Katlian and the invasion of the Russians.

Katlian knew an attack was imminent and ultimately led the attack against the invading force, making him legendary.

He had been working in the new fort. It was nearing the end of summer. Fish had been caught and were being processed and stored for the winter months, drying on racks outside the fort. Likewise, deer meat and hides.

Katlian's scouts had gotten information that Lord Baranov himself and a group of boats had left Kodiak and were enroute to Sitka. He had anticipated this day and felt a rush of adrenaline.

Katlian came to the front of the fort and looked out at the water. He could not see anything. He and Kix got in a canoe that was on the shore and quickly paddled to their other camp; that included a small fort atop of a hill that would later be known as Castle Hill. He quickly climbed the trail up the hill to get a better view of the water.

On top of Castle Hill was a commanding view of the waters surrounding Sitka. He met with the scout, and Katlian squinted in the direction the scout pointed. He could see the shapes— dots, really—of several vessels, miles out to sea yet. One of the dots was larger than the rest. The warship Neva.

"Keep a watch!" he said and began to put in motion plans that had been made for the return of the Russians.

Kix and Katlian returned to the main camp. Word had traveled and leaders were gathering in the fort. An emergency meeting of the Tribal leaders would happen shortly. Meanwhile, Katlian issued orders to people under his command. It appeared the Russian flotilla was bypassing their location, the Tlingit main camp, and was instead heading north, probably the seven miles or so to another of the previous Russian camp sites.

"Katlian defeated them before. He can defeat them again," one of the clan leaders had said to the assembled group.

"It is true, but that was without their Chief Baranof, and was against a small force he left behind," another leader spoke.

"The Russians first came here many seasons ago looking for hunting grounds. At first, it was simply smaller boats. They were also willing to trade with us. It worked well for us, as the Russians appeared to be just another foreign Tribe. They had valuable things to trade for pelts, which was good for us. We had enough furs to trade, and there seem to be plenty for all, so it was not a problem at first," Shaman Stoon continued.

"We have traded with outside Tribes in the past; this was not new. We have traded with English or other groups before. We traded for things they have that are valuable to us. Knives that are stronger and better than ours, buttons, cloth that is different and lighter than our skins, but better than the reeds we used. It was a good at first, with not too much conflict. Things changed, as we all know."

The Russian settlement several miles north had been called Old Harbor or Saint Michaels. It was more like a small town and included residences for Baranof and the crews, a warehouse to store trading goods or other things, a blacksmith shop, cattle sheds, even a bathhouse. The Tlingit had had enough; relations with the Russians deteriorated. The Tlingit then attacked Saint Michaels several times, but with limited success.

Katlian had fearlessly stormed the small community, using a two-pound sledge he had found to crush the skull of one man and batter countless Aleut warriors siding with the Russians. The attack was a huge success for the Tlingit's and was a major factor in Katlian's rise in status in the Tribe.

CHAPTER 7
KATLIAN

The next night Chief Snow again met Lanny Brady at her home near the police academy. It had turned out that she only lived a couple short blocks from the academy, so it had been very convenient for Snow to visit her.

They both seemed to enjoy each other's company, and Lanny liked to hear about life in the village. She liked to hear about his job as a police chief as well and was forming a judgment about what kind of policeman he was. Lanny, like most Natives, had a long and well-deserved distrust of the police. It seemed as if the police were all too willing to throw a Tribal citizen in jail, but it appeared White folks got better treatment, or at least benefit of the doubt. Statistics proved that Tribal people represented a disproportionately high number of people in jail. The distaste aimed at cops stemmed from a multi-generational mistreatment of Natives.

It seemed like Natives had to fight for everything, even the things that White people took for granted. Like the right to be treated with some respect. As Lanny talked and listened to Chief Snow, she took the opportunity to try and educate him on those realities. But she also felt that he seemed to understand what she was talking about. She was hopeful, anyway, especially with his involvement with the Tribal Court.

"Tonight, we go for a little walk," she said. The weather was sunny and mild, so it was a good night for a walk.

"Sounds good," Snow agreed, and they set off.

When they got down to the water by Lincoln Street, Lanny turned south. They walked on the sidewalk and passed the old Sheldon Jackson campus and eventually stopped in front of Totem Park, as the locals called the National Historical Park in downtown Sitka. She led him to the beach, and they found a promising large log to sit on. They both lit up.

"It was right here," Lanny said after a minute.

"What was right here?" Snow asked.

"This is where the old fort was located," she said, motioning off to her left, the long cigarette in her fingers like a pointer. "*Shís'gi Noow,* the fort that the Shaman Stoon encouraged the Kiksadi to build, was right here."

"Wow! I am impressed, Lanny!" Snow said.

"Katlian and Nami may have sat right in this very spot," she said with a kind of reverence. "My ancestors. Your ancestors," she said.

"So, you going to tell me what happened? How the story ends?" Snow asked.

"Yes. And it happened right here in front of where we now sit," she said.

■ ■ ■

"We must withdraw!" Shaman Stoon said passionately.

The Shaman was dressed in his formal clothing including the headdress he wore on special occasions. Though he was completely filthy, he still cut an impressive figure. The shaman never bathed, as was custom. But his clothing appeared pristine. He was wearing a robe that had Tribal symbols and was dyed red and black. He also wore the tall headdress made of skins wrapped around small twigs. The ends of the twigs poked up from the headdress making it appear even taller. He had a carved rattle attached to his right hand by a leather strap. Sometimes, when he used his hands to make a point, the rattle would make subtle noises.

A meeting had materialized after a disastrous explosion within the fort that had killed off a number of the warriors and leaders.

Shaman Stoon continued. "It is a bad omen, I think. We must assume it is so and take it as a sign that we cannot win a fight against the Russians."

No one could deny that it was a horrible incident. To say that the Tlingit should surrender or withdraw was what most people were thinking at this point. It was a bad thing on a number of different levels.

"The Russians will expect us to do that," Katlian said. But he did not elaborate on what he was thinking.

"We lost most of our gunpowder in the explosion. We lost any reserve supply we had, not just of gunpowder but the extra balls, and muskets. Stoon is right, I think," another Elder spoke deliberately and slowly, as if he had given this a lot of thought.

"We should stick to our original plan. We should assess their strength of arms and men, then make a decision as Katlian suggested before. We still are not fully aware of their strength or their intentions," the same Elder said.

"I would say their intentions are clear," Stoon said. "They mean to make war against us as demonstrated by their attacks, and the explosion that killed so many of our leaders and destroyed the supplies needed to defend ourselves."

"The Russians were simply trying to harass or impede our canoes from coming and going. It was unfortunate that the explosion happened, but I say we should wait and see what the Russians have to say, what they intend," the Elder spoke again, but it appeared that was all he was going to say.

"It is true that the Russian usually will make contact. I expect they will send an emissary to relate to us their intentions," Katlian said.

"They want our land, our camps at this and other locations. They want all the pelts they can get. And they want our women as well," another respected Elder spoke. "They have already taken some of our women; they want everything they can get."

Stoon continued to lobby for leaving. "I say we should leave now as we had talked about doing if their numbers were too great. We had a plan that if the situation called for it, we would retreat to one of our winter camps to avoid potential defeat to the Russians. We are in that situation now!" Stoon declared.

A number of conversations sparked, and the meeting devolved into chaos with sidebars and separate conversations, and in general, everyone seeming to talk at the same time.

A warrior rushed in, and the room hushed as he delivered news.

"They are towing the warship into the bay. It appears they mean to position it to fire at this fort," the warrior said.

The room again exploded, with everyone talking at once.

Katlian thought about his conversation with Nami earlier. She was distraught over the loss of the men, in particular Kix, Katlian's good friend and close confidant. She was grieving not only for the men lost, but also for her husband. She knew how much Katlian loved and valued his friend Kix.

"I wish the Russians had never come to this place," she said to Katlian.

"Yes. Me too. But wishing won't make it so. They are here and want what is ours," he said.

"But why? They have their ships. They can go anywhere. Why must they come here to our home?" she said, not really expecting an answer. She was frustrated and needed to express it.

"I don't know if we have the warriors to fight them now," Katlian said. "It is not just the numbers of men, it is the leadership and the shadow that has been cast over the Kiksadi, losing the men in that way."

"I can fight. I want to fight, you need warriors, you say, but I am right here and want to fight!" Nami said and stood. She went to the corner and grabbed one of the spears and held it in her hands.

Back at the meeting, the same warrior entered, and the room got quiet. "There is a boat coming to shore, under flag of truce," he announced.

An emissary!

"I will see what they have to say!" Katlian announced. No one disagreed and he stepped out of the fort. He saw Nami and motioned for her. She lay down the spear.

"I want you to come with me. You understand some of the Russian, better than I do. It may be helpful to have you there to also hear what is said," he said to her. She nodded and they began to walk to the beach.

A large wooden rowboat was being paddled toward their location. There was a tall Russian man in uniform standing at the front. Behind him was a woman, something of a surprise. He had a white rag tied to a musket and was holding it aloft. It was dark and misting rain. An Aleut warrior held a torch aloft which was how the Tlingit's had spotted them coming.

Katlian and Nami were at the front of a group that had come to meet the boat on the shore in front of the Tlingit fort, Shís'gi Noow. Behind them was a group of warriors who were armed and ready to engage.

Katlian was dressed in his ceremonial battle gear. He was wearing a light colored soft tanned deer hide garment that went to just above his knees. The under garment was overlaid by a vest that was made of thin slats of wood, held together with strings made woven from tough reeds. This vest could stop a musket ball, though not at close range. The vests were often decorated with painted or carved clan symbols and were particular to the warrior. Over top, he was wearing a cloak of wolf hide, a prized garment that was warm but also very distinctive looking. The cloak could be held together by a tie made of string in the front. Katlian held his sledge in his right hand, the same hammer he had taken from the first raid.

He wore his war helmet. Like the vest, his warrior helmet was one he had fashioned himself, with help from Nami. Katlian had more than one helmet, however. The one he wore tonight left his face exposed. It was fashioned from reeds and small twigs and was covered with fur. On the helmet was a carved raven beak and eyes pointing forward. The beak had been darkened and appeared realistic and distinctive. Around his neck, he wore another protective collar, meant to protect his neck from a knife or stray ball. It was also decorated with Tribal symbols.

The Russian dropped out of the front of the boat and onto the sand. He helped the woman out of the boat.

"That's enough; only you two need to get out!" Katlian spoke Tlingit to the Russian. The woman next to him quickly translated.

The Russian solider turned to face Chief Katlian. He straightened up his uniform by pulling the outer coat down in front. It was a dark colored uniform, complete with brass buttons in front and a gold braid on the shoulders. He had a bicorn naval captain's hat on his head which pointed forward and back. This hat signified that he was a ship's captain. He wore a long sword in a scabbard by his right side. Katlian paid the sword particular attention. He would have liked to hold it in his hands and examine it.

Captain Lisianski was tall, thin, and handsome. He was in dress uniform and removed his hat in a sweeping gesture, placing it under his left arm. His hair was dark brown but had been trimmed up short. He sported heavy mutton chop style sideburns but was otherwise clean shaven.

"Captain Yuri Lisianski of the Russian Imperial Navy. Captain of the Neva. I bring word from Lord Baranof," Lisianski stated in Russian. This was translated into Tlingit by the woman at Lisianski's left. Lisianski noticed Katlian's hammer.

The woman was a Tlingit. She had been taken as a wife by Lisianski. She was a beautiful young Native woman in a Russian dress. She was fluent in Russian.

It was somewhat unusual for combatants to meet outside the field of battle, especially two of the top military leaders of their respective groups. It was more typical to send lower-level representatives to meet and discuss terms. But Lisianski was not your typical naval captain. He was world traveled and liked to be out front. In particular, he knew that indigenous groups expected an emissary to be a leader, and to be impressive.

Another unusual aspect was to have two women directly involved in the meeting of the military leaders, as women were usually in the background.

"I am Katlian of the Kiksadi," Katlian responded by giving his lineage. This was customary during introductions in Tlingit. At times, an introduction could take several minutes. But Katlian gave a shortened version. He was a naturally impatient man.

After the formalities were over, Captain Lisianski spoke.

"Lord Baranof is seeking compensation for the attack and looting of our Saint Michael's camp. He wants to use the Noow Tlein site as our new base of operations. It is our understanding that the Tlingit have used the site on the hill in the past. But now we demand access to this site by way of compensation for the unwarranted attack at Saint Michaels," Lisianski demanded.

Nami whispered into Katlian's ear. "Don't agree to anything, Kut." Of course, Katlian was familiar with negotiations and understood this basic principle. He would not and could not make any sort of deal with the Russians in this instance, unless it was an extraordinarily good deal for the Tlingit. Even then he would likely not agree to anything, until he had brought it to the Tribal leaders. In this instance, what the Russians were demanding was not even in the vicinity of being a good deal for the Tlingit's.

"If the Tlingit do not accept this offer, we will begin the cannon bombardment of the Tlingit fort forthwith." Lisianski threatened, referring to the fort behind Katlian by raising his arm in that direction.

Katlian understood the nature of this type of negotiation and understood there was a time to be diplomatic and a time to push. He pushed.

"Why is Baranof not here himself, but instead sends a boy to do his speaking for him? Is your Lord too frightened to appear in person?!" Katlian said, in Russian.

Lisianski's wife was startled, but the captain grinned and replied to Katlian in Tlingit.

"You and I are indeed errand boys today. We were chosen I believe, because of our standing in our Tribes. You are the great war Chief Katlian of the Kiksadi. I am captain of the Royal Russian Navy. But today, it is true that we are not on the battlefield against one another. Today, it is our trusted duty to simply deliver the important messages to our leaders, for them to decide upon and to take action," Lisianski stated smoothly.

Lisianski reverted back to his native tongue. "We made an agreement with the Tlingit. We paid for access to these hunting grounds. The Tlingit broke our agreement by attacking our camp at Saint Michaels. We seek reparations for your violation of our agreement. We feel that the camp on the hill would be *just compensation. We would prefer not to go to war but are prepared to do so as I indicated."*

"If you do not want war, why do you say you will begin firing your cannons at us?" Katlian asked but did not wait for an answer.

"The Russians were not honest in their negotiations with us. YOU violated the agreement by demanding labor from us for your Czar. And by taking our women! This was not part of the agreement we made with the Russians. We attacked your fort in compensation for your violation of the agreement," Katlian said and pointed at the woman doing the translation for Lisianski as evidence.

The captain understood that loss of their women to the Russians by any means could be an affront to the Tlingit's. Wars had been started and been fought for exactly this issue, he mused.

"I am sure there may have been transgressions of the agreement by both sides. But I will say this, the woman at my side is my wife. I did not take her; she is with me by choice, of her free will," he said, looking over at his wife, Tess. She looked at her husband as she translated back to Katlian. Her eyes said it was true; she was with Lisianski by her choice.

"Your soldiers hunt and trap more than is needed, more than you said you would in the original agreement, and nothing was ever said about the Tlingit serving your master, the Czar," Katlian said in his language.

"Perhaps that is true. It may be time to meet and negotiate a new agreement. In any case, let me again state the message I was told to deliver. Cede the Noow Tlein camp site on the hill to Lord Baranof. We will begin bombardment of your fort until we receive an answer. My duty is complete, we await your answer," Lisianski said again in a way that suggested the meeting was over. After he was done talking, he indicated to Katlian that they were going to leave now. He held his arm for

Tess to clamber back aboard the large rowboat. And then he pushed the boat off the beach and neatly jumped aboard.

Katlian gave orders to his warriors. They covered the beach as he and Nami turned to walk back to the fort. The meeting was over.

■ ■ ■

The sun was starting to go down on the site by Totem Park in Sitka where Lanny and Snow were sitting on a log near the beach. Snow had been imagining the meeting between Chief Katlian and Captain Lisianski taking place right here in front of him as Lanny told the story. Lanny had stopped talking; it seemed like a natural break in her account.

"These men were both pretty impressive! Especially Katlian, he was a very clever man, I think. I can see why he was a chief," Snow said as they both lit up a smoke.

"That is true. I think many people simply view Katlian as a great warrior, an accomplished fighter, and leader of other warriors. But I believe there was much more to him than that," Lanny said.

"Lisianski seems like a formidable rival," Snow said.

"Yes, I think that is also true. He was a man of many accomplishments and talents," Lanny paused. "I need a bathroom break," she said. They both got up and walked back the way they had come to Lanny's house.

"I have to leave in the morning," Snow told his newfound mother. "I need to get back to the village and then fly to Anchorage with my deputy and, um . . . my woman friend. We're trying to find a missing girl."

"I understand . . . son," Lanny smiled. "When you're done with your business there, come back, and I'll finish telling you about your past."

CHAPTER 8
ANCHOR TOWN

The day after his return from Sitka, Chief Snow, Lilly Wassillie, and Stanley Beans were on the jet heading to Anchorage.

The chief was lost in thought as the plane droned on toward Anchorage. Before leaving, he had reached out to Tom Begich first, which was a bit unusual. Normally he probably would have called the Anchorage Police Department (APD) or troopers first. But he felt more comfortable calling Tom, who had arranged for him to meet with a Detective Ramos when he got into town.

Lilly was thinking about Mary Frank. She was worried about her cousin and hoped she was simply checking out the big city. Maybe got caught up in the party scene, which often happened to folks from the village when they hit the big town. She wanted to help Mary get out of there before anything bad happened.

Lilly showed Chief Snow a picture on her phone of Mary Frank.

"I remember her," Snow said. "I talked to her one night when she was out late. It was nothing, really, but she was out past curfew. I kept thinking there was more to why she was out at night like that."

"I think she started getting mixed up with adults drinking, getting, um, you know, *active.*"

Snow looked at Lilly and understood what she meant.

"You don't think she was being sexually abused, do you?" Snow asked.

"She did not give any indication of that when I talked to her at the clinic. But something was not right. I could tell. At the time, I thought she was simply worried about possibly getting pregnant. Could have been more to it, though, I am thinking now. I should have done more."

"You did what you could. You can't read minds," Snow said to comfort her.

"I mean, I tried, you know? I wanted her to talk to me, because I could tell there was more to it, but she was defensive or distrustful . . . something," Lilly said. "I should have tried harder!"

"We will find her," Snow said.

The Alaska Airlines jet banked over Cook Inlet to make the approach toward the airport that abutted the water. Mount Susitna, or Sleeping Lady, was visible, complete with a blanket of snow to the west. There was water below the plane, but also a lot of sand. Cook Inlet had some of the largest tides in the world—at low tide, a mass of sand and mud. The tides ran like a river back in to fill the inlet and were not for the faint of heart to navigate.

Anchorage was the biggest city in Alaska at about 280,000 souls, which amounted to somewhat less than half the state's total population. Anchorage was not only the biggest city in Alaska, but it also served as a hub for shopping, medical, airlines, and just about any other services you could not get in the bush.

Anchorage had the bustle of a hub city or border town. There were a lot of bars and strip clubs catering to the men that worked the fisheries, the oil patch, and other male dominated blue-collar industries. There were also bars that tended to serve the Native population primarily.

It was ironic that the 4th Avenue strip was a tourist hot spot during summer days, even though the bars were rough and tumble and the downtown parks usually had homeless people and chronic alcoholics panhandling or sleeping it off. The city had attempted to clean things up, but the problems persisted.

After retrieving their luggage in the newly remodeled and spacious airport terminal, the trio went down to get a rental car, which was in rough shape and strewn with trash inside. It would do, though, and perhaps draw less attention driving around a new vehicle while searching for Mary Frank. God only knew what parts of town they may have to look for her.

Snow drove since he had the most knowledge of Anchorage. But Stanley and Lilly were no stranger to the big town. Both had spent extensive time there shopping or for a medical visit, or simply passing through, as was the case for most Alaskans. Snow got directions from Stanley to the place they would be staying. One of the Togiak Council members had a small place near the airport that had been arranged for them to use should they need it.

"Turn here!" Stanley said after they had passed through an intersection on Tudor Road. Snow went up the next intersection and made a U-turn back toward the airport.

"Eeee, this is the place!" Stanley said, pointing to a shack on the left as Snow drove through a decrepit looking neighborhood strewn with junk vehicles and ramshackle homes. But even they looked good compared to the shack Stanley pointed to.

"Oh, dear God! I hope the inside is better than the outside!" Lilly said.

"Don't worry, it's nice. I mean it has everything in it," Stanley said, which did nothing to assuage Lilly's anxiety.

The driveway was snow covered, but they were able to find a spot to park without getting stuck. Weeds stuck up through the snow. Stanley found the key on a nail in the lean-to next to the main house. He opened the door and led the way.

Inside, it was warm, which was the best that could be said about it. The place was small. The front door emptied into the kitchen/living room. You could see a bedroom that had a small bathroom. That was it. It was not much bigger than a hotel room, and certainly a lot seedier.

Lilly went back and checked the bathroom. She did not make any sounds or say anything. *That could be good or bad,* thought Snow. He was checking to make sure the water was on. There was even hot water—a good sign, for sure. Stanley had his head in the refrigerator for a couple seconds, but there was nothing to see in there except an old bottle of ketchup. Stanley opened and shut most of the drawers in the kitchen.

"See, we got forks, knives, pots, and pans. The stove works. It's got everything we need!" Stanley said.

Lilly came out of the bedroom and looked ill.

"I don't know about this. I mean, I am not sure I want to stay here," she frowned. Snow was feeling the same way. Stanley had turned on the ancient TV and all were surprised that it worked and something was actually on the screen. It looked like a local channel.

"It's not so bad!" Stanley said. "We got TV!"

Lilly and Snow exchanged a look. Snow moved in and gave Lilly a long hug, because at that moment, she seemed to need one.

"We can get a hotel if you want, Lilly," Snow said quietly to her.

She moved her head back and forth, surveying the little house, not speaking for a minute or two.

"I guess we can try it, but it stinks in here!" she said.

Snow sniffled a bit and it did smell kind of musty, with a rotten undertone. But to him, the smell was the least offensive part of the place. He was worried about the bed, and maybe bed bugs. He had not seen sign of roaches or rats yet. *Maybe they had all moved to a better location,* thought Snow. The neighborhood looked like a demilitarized zone. Snow had been in worse, and this was a working trip, not a pleasure cruise.

"We will try it together. Deputy Beans, you have the couch!" Snow ordered. The sofa was not much bigger than a love seat and was a dirty yellow in color.

"Eeee, Chief. I got it!" Stanley appeared quite pleased.

That night, Lilly did some cleaning, especially the bathroom. They had all gone to the big Carrs grocery store up the street for supplies and food. The store was nice. It even had a salad bar and deli. This was living in the city! In the village, fresh food was a luxury. And there were restaurants—real ones, not just camp chili or burgers.

"I want to go to Kentucky Fried Chicken, KFC! I love their gravy," Stanley said.

"I have a craving for a Quarter Pounder with Cheese from McDonald's!" Lilly said.

"I am sure we can hit one of those places. I need to meet up with a Detective Alex Ramos tonight. I think both of you should come in case there are questions about Mary. We can hit one of those joints or both, either before or after," Snow said.

"There is a Micky D's right up the street by the Carrs store, and a KFC just a few blocks away on Northern Lights," Snow continued.

"Where are we meeting this detective guy?" Lilly asked.

"I have an address. I am supposed to meet him at nine," Snow said.

They decided to rest for a bit before heading out. Traveling made them tired. Snow and Lilly lay on top of the bed in their clothes with an old wool blanket covering them. Even though the place was a dump, it felt nice.

"I wanted to take you to someplace nice, you know. Like the Captain Cook or the Hilton downtown. I know of a good Japanese restaurant downtown. I think it is called Kumagoro's; I wanted to take you," he whispered to Lilly.

"I don't care, as long as we are together," she said to him, putting her hands on his face.

"I love you, Lilly Wassillie!" Snow whispered.

"I know!" Lilly smiled. They snuggled in for a short nap to recharge.

■ ■ ■

After everyone had a bit of rest, they got up and got moving to their meeting. Snow drove directly to the address he had, and it turned out to be a small APD substation in Spenard, not that far away from where they were staying.

They had to get buzzed in and were met by a uniformed officer who led them into a meeting room.

"Tom!" Snow said to Senator Tom Begich who was chatting with a woman. "You look different! Respectable!"

Senator Begich had gotten a haircut recently. His salt-and-pepper hair was trimmed, and he was sporting a goatee. He was slender and about the same height as Chief Snow. He was wearing jeans and a kind of blazer of some sort, and a fedora!

"Chief Snow," Tom responded, and they shook hands. "You look as disheveled as usual," Tom joked.

"What the heck are you doing here? I mean, I know you started this task force, but I did not think a senator would be working in the field with the cops," Snow said.

"I am a licensed private investigator and thought I may be able to help," Tom said.

"Let me introduce you to Detective Alex Ramos. She is on loan from APD and is leading a sex trafficking task force for the Department of Public Safety," Tom said.

Chief Snow's eyebrows fluttered. In his mind, he had expected an old white guy, maybe with a paunch and bald head, kind of the stereotypical cop. Instead, he was shaking the hand of Alex Ramos. She wore skinny black jeans, a black leather coat, and black combat boots. She was young and very pretty, with a brown complexion, dark hair, and liquid brown eyes. Her hair was pulled back tight into a ponytail. She showed her brilliant white teeth, but it was not a smile.

Detective Alex Ramos was a good cop and was a fast riser. She had been heavily impacted by her father who was military stationed at JBER, the Joint Base Elmendorf Richardson in Anchorage. He was tough and no nonsense. Alex had the same qualities, which served her well working in law enforcement, a male dominant environment. She did not take any guff. And she was tough physically as well, finishing at the top of her class in the academy.

One underlying motivation for Detective Ramos was that she had been sexually assaulted as a teenager. That experience created a strong desire in her to hold men accountable that preyed on women, in particular those who preyed on young women. It was like she was on a mission.

In this moment, Alex seemed angry or at the least had a giant chip on her shoulder. It seemed clear by her demeanor that she was not impressed by the rubes from the village. She had her hands on her hips and displayed an attitude from the get-go.

"You were supposed to come here by yourself," she said accusingly to Snow after they shook hands brusquely.

"That's news to me. These are my friends from Togiak. They are here to help search for Mary Frank, and may have helpful information," Snow said.

"What makes you think you can come to my town and start fucking around, probably fucking up investigations we have going on," she admonished. There was a hush and a chill in the air.

Lilly had enough of Alex and her tough girl act, including the profanity. Though Lilly was soft spoken and appeared to be shy, she was unafraid to speak her mind. She often shocked Snow by her directness, saying things that he wanted to say but didn't for fear of offending people. Lilly had a way of speaking the truth that usually did not upset people. He was not sure how she did it.

But she was not being the diplomat this time.

"I am Mary Frank's cousin, and I am here to help look for her. I don't like your attitude or your filthy language. This is not *your* town. If you can't help us, just say so, but don't waste our time!" Lilly scolded. *Shots fired.*

Alex's eyes grew wide, and she fired back, though her aim was at Snow.

"Better get your GF on a leash, Snow. I got no time for this shit!" Even though Alex's comments had been directed to Chief Snow, the two women had closed space and were now standing facing each other, each staring holes in the other.

Girlfriend? thought Snow. *Does it show?*

"Wait, wait, wait," Snow said calmly, stepping between the two women who had squared off. Lilly spun on her heel and backed away. She appeared to be ready to leave. Snow had never seen her this angry. Something about Alex had really set her off.

Snow had been around enough cops to recognize one peeing on the corners, marking territory. He knew he needed to calm the water to salvage the situation before things went totally sideways.

"This is my fault," Snow said, falling on the sword. "I did not know I was supposed to come alone. We have no intention of interfering with any investigation you have going on. We are here to search for one missing girl from our village, Mary Frank, from Togiak. Lilly and my deputy, Stanley Beans, may have helpful information. We are simply seeking your help, and I am sorry, I did not mean to offend you, Detective Ramos."

Snow paused, waiting for cooler heads to prevail.

"Lilly Wassillie is Mary Frank's cousin, and she has a picture and other information on her phone. We would really appreciate any information or help you can offer. You have a good eye, Detective Ramos. Lilly is my girlfriend," Chief Snow said, hoping to toss Alex a bone and settle her down a bit. He thought she was probably just doing the thing cops do—going hard, pushing buttons.

"Stanley Beans works for me as an Emergency Jail Guard and a nonsworn deputy. He knows Anchorage and has some experience around the homeless camps, where Mary may be," Snow explained, treading lightly.

Tom Begich had been sitting back on a counter along the wall checking his phone, apparently ignoring the drama that was playing out. But now he stood up and spoke, taking charge.

"We are all on the same team here. I brought you together because I have a concern that Mary Frank may have gotten swept up into a sex trafficking ring. That is Detective Ramos' bailiwick. I don't need to remind anyone that Native girls are often targeted by bad actors who will drug them and turn them into prostitutes. Village girls are particularly vulnerable. I know this. You know this. I spent a lot of time and energy pushing to create this task force. And I recommended Detective Ramos to lead it because she is passionate about it and an excellent investigator. She has put a lot of bad guys in jail and helped a lot of young women get out of a bad situation. Let's figure out a way to work together on this. Please," Tom said.

"Okay, okay, let me see the picture of the girl," Alex said impatiently. She stepped toward Lilly and asked her with a faint trace of politeness in her voice. "May I see the picture on your phone, Ms. Wassillie?"

Lilly pulled up the picture on her phone and handed it to Alex. She did not say anything, still agitated.

"Thank you, Lilly," Alex said, seeming to soften. She looked at the picture for a minute, seeming to search her memory for any recognition.

"She looks familiar, but I can't be sure. Do you mind if I forward this to my phone?" she asked Lilly.

"Go ahead. It's your town," Lilly responded, still salty. Alex grinned as if amused. After a minute, Alex handed the phone back but stood there for a minute in front of Lilly, looking her up and down. Lilly stared back.

"I think I could use you. Would you be willing to work for me if we find out this girl is working for one of our traffickers?" Alex asked, speaking now directly to Lilly.

"I'll do anything I can to help! But I will only work if Brady is involved," she replied.

"Who the fuck is Brady?" Alex said.

"I the fuck am Brady," said Snow with a smile.

"Wait a minute. If you are saying what I think you're saying, I think the answer is a hard no. If you are talking about Lilly going under cover, then no, hell no!" Snow said to Alex.

"She's perfect, though. She is pretty, young, and Native. And I suspect she is older than she looks if she is shacking up with you," Alex said.

It was Chief Snow's cue to push back. Snow walked up to stand in front of Detective Ramos. No nonsense now.

"We want your help, but you have stepped over the line now, twice. We can walk out of here now, but if we stay, you will show some respect. Or you and I are going to have a serious Come to Jesus event." He had enough of her mouth and attitude. And when it came to Lilly, he was protective. He stared hard at her, and she stared back, until she finally looked away.

Alex spoke to the room. "I deal with assholes and dirtbags 24/7. I have seen things, bad things, that makes me a bit of a hard case sometimes. I sometimes forget there are good people, normal, left in the world. But Senator Begich is right about one thing, I am passionate about this shit, and am good at it. So anyway, I am sorry if I came on too strong," Alex said.

"I think you meant to say, *like a bitch*," Lilly said. But she said it as a joke, and it came off that way. Everyone smiled a bit and relaxed.

"I like her!" Alex said to the room, smiling at Lilly.

Tom Begich spoke again. "Detective Ramos, Chief Snow has worked a lot of sex cases in the bush, I mean *a lot*. It is part of the reason I set up this meeting. He worked cases that I know most village cops would have backed away from. He knows what goes on and I think he could be helpful to you."

"Okay, then. Let's get down to business. We're burning daylight," said Alex. Chief Snow smiled at that.

CHAPTER 9

BEANS

Detective Alex Ramos helped the Togiak Trio develop a plan of action. Alex had some ideas about what to do if they could not find the missing sixteen-year-old Mary Frank. She had reached out to the hospitals and shelters in Anchorage to ensure all bases were covered. After a night's sleep in their plywood palace, the three started their quest.

"Let's review our list of things to do, places to check," Snow said.

"How about Bean's café first?" Stanley offered. "Maybe we can get some breakfast!"

Beans Café was actually a very large food kitchen adjacent to the Brother Francis Homeless Shelter just off 3rd Avenue downtown. Even though it was a homeless shelter, everyone just called it Beans. At certain times, dozens of people could be seen in the area smoking or milling about. Stanley Bean had no relation to the name of the food kitchen.

They climbed in the battered rental car as they left their dingy abode. He got on Minnesota Avenue and took it all the way to the downtown area where he headed east on 4th Avenue through the bar, hotel, and restaurant district. They drove past the Captain Cook Hotel as well as the Hilton Tower and other landmarks. They also passed several well-known watering holes such as the Gaslamp, the Pioneer Bar, and the Avenue. Despite the proximity to luxury hotels and shopping, some of the bars were quite rough. It was a curiosity that so many were located just blocks from Beans Café and the homeless shelter. At one time, downtown Anchorage was rife with strip clubs and prostitutes, but that had changed some years ago, in an effort to clean things up for the tourists.

"The Bush Company used to be right there," Stanley pointed. Bush was perhaps the most famous of all the notorious strip bars in Anchorage. It was still in business but had moved to a location out by the airport. There were no longer exotic dance clubs in the downtown district. They had all been dispersed around various parts of town, such as midtown or the Spenard area. As the downtown area started to thin out, Snow took a left at the intersection where 4th Avenue bent north toward Ship Creek and crossed 3rd Avenue. He went back a half a block or so toward downtown.

The trio walked into Beans Café. Inside the main door was a large open area with long rows of tables set up, ready for customers. There was a smattering of people at various tables, most sitting in groups. Someone waved and Stanley peeled off and headed toward a group sitting at one of the long tables.

There was a long serving line that ran parallel to the tables. Several people were standing behind the line, waiting for someone to come up that needed food. It seemed that the breakfast period was about over. Stanley suddenly appeared in line to get some food!

"Wanna get some food?" Snow asked Lilly with a smirk.

"I think I'm good," Lilly responded, her nose wrinkled up disapprovingly. "It stinks in here."

Snow could not smell anything but coffee. That was not unusual though. Often Lilly smelled things that he didn't until later, and often certain smells really bothered her.

"The coffee smells good. I'm going to get some. C'mon, Lilly!" Snow said. He grabbed her hand and led her toward the end of the serving line where there were cups and drinks and a couple giant coffee pots. Stanley had gotten food and rejoined a group of people sitting at one of the tables.

"The glasses look dirty," Lilly said, picking one up off a tray and holding it up to the light. Snow gave her a napkin and she wiped the glass before getting some orange juice. Snow got some coffee and sipped it before adding cream and sugar.

"Coffee is okay, though a little weak for my taste."

"The orange juice is actually good," Lilly remarked.

The two went up to the counter and Snow asked to speak to someone in charge.

A tall woman in a nun's habit came out to greet them. Her name was Sister Vickie, and she was very helpful and talkative. She had an easy smile and exuded a happy upbeat vibe. Snow had printed out some fliers with info and the picture of Mary Frank on it, with his contact information to call. He talked to the sister.

"Usually, the young women don't come here too much, as you can see," Sister Vickie said and gestured toward the tables. It was true that the vast majority of the people were men, with a couple older women in the mix.

"Any idea where we could look for her?" Lilly asked.

"I would check the women's shelter in midtown. The shelter is for rape victims, or victims of domestic violence. But unfortunately, that is just about everybody," Sister Vickie lamented.

"How do you manage to stay so upbeat?" Lilly asked. "I think I would be super depressed if I did your job."

Sister Vickie laughed boisterously.

"Oh, honey, you just got to look on the bright side of things!" Sister Vickie said with enthusiasm. "I mean, if you think about it, we all start from scratch every day we get up and get out of bed, right?" Lilly looked unconvinced.

Sister Vickie put her arm around the much shorter Lilly and gave her a sideways hug.

"Life is short, Lilly. You gotta grab it by the short hairs and go for it!" Sister Vickie said with a wicked smile.

"You're not like any of the nuns I know, Sister Vickie, and I mean that in a good way!" Chief Snow said.

"Call me Vic. I was not always a nun, you know," she said, grinning.

"I am worried about my cousin, Mary, you know, Vic. She could be in trouble or worse," Lilly said with emotion.

"We'll find her. If she is anything like you, she is tough, and she will make it!" Sister Vickie said, squeezing Lilly with the arm that was over her shoulder. "C'mon honey, let's sit down for a spell."

Sister Vickie led them to one of the many open tables in the main dining hall and they all sat for a bit and chatted. Snow looked over to check on Stanley who looked content in his element.

Sister Vickie talked about herself for a few minutes. She had worked long as a victim's advocate, and it seemed clear that she had been a victim herself, though she never came out and said as much. It just seemed to be there under the surface. She turned her attention to the matter at hand.

"I don't need to tell you, but I will anyway. These chicks that come in from the village may be a bit naïve at first when they hit town. And they can certainly be exploited. But these Native village chicks are tough. I saw one chick drop some guy with a right cross to the nose for pawing at her. Dropped him like a bad habit," Sister Vickie said with a smile.

"They are survivors. We are all survivors," Lilly said.

After a few more minutes, Sister Vickie got up and left them in her wake, off to do good works for others. She had promised to call Chief Snow's number if Mary Frank turned up, or if she got any information.

"If she wasn't a nun, I would say she was hitting on you, Brady," Lilly teased. Snow practically spit out his coffee, then waved to Stanley to join them.

"Find out anything, Deputy Beans?"

"Eeee. I met some folks I know, most from around Bethel. But one from Togiak, too. He knows Mary and said he has seen her, but not here. He saw her in a camp up by midtown where he was before he moved here. I mean, he moved to a camp nearby, in Ship Creek woods."

"Do you know that camp, Stanley, the one by midtown?" Lilly asked.

"Eeee. I been there before," Stanley said.

"Okay then," Snow said, and they all got up to leave.

"As long as we are downtown, let's go check out the mall, see if Mary is walking around there," Lilly said. Stanley and Snow looked at each other and made big eyes, but neither said anything.

■ ■ ■

The 5th Avenue mall was only a few blocks away. Lilly led the two men around as she ostensibly looked for Mary. This was fine with the two men, because truth be told, both enjoyed being at a shopping mall for a change. Nothing like it in the village, that was for sure.

Snow checked his phone and then called Detective Ramos as Lilly shopped around in women's clothing stores.

"Hey, I am downtown. I will meet you at the food court in about thirty to give you an update," Alex said.

They met at the food court, which is on the top floor of the mall. Half the ceiling was a sky light; it was a pleasant place to sit and have a bite. Snow did not immediately recognize Alex as she walked up to them. She had on jeans and had her hair down. She almost looked like a teenager. Snow wondered where she kept her firearm.

"Who are you and what have you done to Detective Ramos?" Snow joked.

Alex smiled and asked if they made any progress.

"We checked Bean's Café and the shelter, talked to a lady named Vic. No luck. But Stanley ran into some people he knows who said she was seen at the midtown homeless camp, but that was at least a week ago."

"Hey, good work, Stanley!" Alex said with a brilliant smile. Stanley beamed shyly. "I know Sister Vickie; she kills me," she added.

"I have some news too. I have a CI that thinks he may have seen your girl in one of the houses," Alex said, referring to a confidential informant. "He's not sure but said he thought it might be her. It is a supposed dating service out in Spenard. Actually, right next door to where we met at the substation."

"The house is run by a Black dude named Jon Brown. Bad actor with gang ties to lower forty-eight," Alex said.

"Check that camp. If you come up empty, give me a call, and we'll meet later," she said.

"You should check out Nordstrom, Lilly. They got a big sale going on!" Alex said as she left.

"Thanks, Alex! Is that where you shop?" Lilly asked.

"Nah, not usually. Too spendy. I actually like going to secondhand stores if I have time. There's usually some good stuff there, if you search. That's where I got this outfit," Alex said.

"Wow! Really. You look great. I can't believe it!" Lilly said. Snow was relieved that the two women had gotten past the rough start when they first met.

The chief let Stanley drive since he knew where the shelter

out in midtown was located. He immediately regretted it. Stanley was a village-only type of driver, and after a couple near misses, he pulled into a gas station off Seward and 9th and parked the battered rental.

"Can you drive, Chief?" Stanley asked. "I am out of practice driving in the big city. Eeee, too many cars!" Stanley said.

"Sure. You can navigate," Snow said, thankful Stanley had pulled over.

"Keep going this way, and take a left at Freddy's," Stanley said.

Snow drove south on Seward, hung a left on Benson, and drove a few blocks, then Stanley told him to find a place to park. Off to their left, there was a lot of tree cover. In fact, Anchorage had a lot of green space. Chester Creek ran through the heart of town and there was greenbelt around it, including a couple small lakes.

They parked, and Stanley led the way as they hoofed it through the woods. There was an obvious path to follow and soon they saw some signs of life. The smell of wood smoke perfumed the air. It was getting on toward late afternoon, and the days were still fairly short this time of the year. It was cool, in the upper twenties. These three were not put off by some cool weather, though. More of a concern was getting in and out before it got full dark. The sun set in the afternoon this time of year, up only about six hours a day.

Alaska is a huge state. The old joke that you could cut Alaska in half and Texas would be the third largest state is true. At 663,268 square miles (1,717,856 km²) in area, Alaska is by far the largest state in the United States, and is more than twice the size of the second-largest U.S. state, Texas. Alaska is the seventh largest subnational division in the world, and if it was an independent nation would be the 16th largest country in the world.

Alaska is also a land of climatic extremes. The cold is a factor in winter but only part of the equation. Alaska is known as the

Land of the Midnight sun, also called White Nights in other parts of the world such as Russia. This is true in the northern part of the state. In Barrow the sun does not set for a couple months, instead circling around the sky. The opposite affect takes place in winter when sunlight can be hard to come by. In Barrow the sun does not rise for almost two months. The periods of extreme darkness can be difficult to adjust to and can cause depression or SAD—seasonal affective disorder.

Anchorage is about sixty-one degrees north a similar latitude as Hudson Bay in Canada. At this time of year Anchorage received around six hours of sunlight. Everyday there would be more light until the middle of summer when the sun would be up for about 18 hours. On this day however, the sun would be setting in the late afternoon.

■ ■ ■

They arrived at a campfire with several people sitting near the fire on some logs that had been positioned for that purpose. The people looked up, and to Snow and Stanley's surprise, they recognized one of the men.

"Tuzzy!" Stanley said joyfully. "What cher doing?"

Bill Tuzzy lived in Togiak and worked for the local air carriers as their ground man. Snow had said before that Bill Tuzzy was the hardest worker in Togiak. And it was true. But right now, he was pretty well cooked by the looks of it.

"Stanley Beans, it's great to see you. I'm not surprised to see you, my friend. But Chief Snow? Well, this is a surprise indeed. And ahh, Lilly Wassillie, right? It is a pleasure to see such fine folks out here in the woods," Tuzzy said.

Although Tuzzy seemed very drunk, swaying as he stood, his speech was clear as a bell.

"We are looking for my cousin, Mary Frank, Tuzzy. She is missing. Maybe you can help us?" Lilly said.

"I talked to a couple guys down at Bean's Café, and they said she was here last week, or at least they saw her here," Stanley added.

Tuzzy sat back down on the log and motioned for them to sit too. He lost his balance as he sat but recovered quickly. He explained that he had been crashing at this site for a few days, and that he had not seen Mary during that time. He knew Mary quite well, though, and had heard she had hooked up with some friends hitting bars and heading downtown to party. That was perhaps a week ago. He didn't know who the friends were, but he had guessed that they went to the Avenue Bar. That was where most of the people around this camp frequented when they went in town, Tuzzy said, after receiving their monthly unemployment or Native Corporation check.

"Lilly and Chief Snow, I can tell you are feeling bad for me. But don't. I am here because I wanted to be with my wife's friends."

Tuzzy's wife had been killed in a tragic whaling accident. The whale was being dragged out of the water and up the beach where it could be butchered. One of the series of cables used to drag the massive whale snapped and hit Tuzzy's wife, killing her instantly. Tuzzy was a White man, but his wife was a local Native. He had stayed in the area despite his loss and became a vital part of the Togiak community. Apparently, spending time in a homeless camp drinking with friends was a respite for him.

■ ■ ■

Snow and Detective Ramos entered Chilkoot Charlie's Bar in Spenard together. Chilkoot Charlie's, or Koots, was a historic bar in Anchorage. It was partially constructed from logs, named after a local radio personality who had gotten the name from the historic Chilkoot pass that was used by miners to get to the gold fields during the Klondike gold rush of the later nineteenth century. Now, it was a large and sprawling club with several sections, offering a variety of entertainment.

They sat on bar stools made from empty kegs of beer and large wooden stumps. Sawdust covered the floor. Alex had called and asked to meet them outside the bar. After getting a sitrep from Snow about their trip to the camp, she explained the situation and the reason for meeting at Koots.

"One of my CI's told me he may have seen Mary Frank in one of the houses here in Spenard. I wanted to hit Koots because the guy who runs that house likes to come here. Sometimes he will recruit girls here or he will bring some of his girls here to troll for Johns. The guy's name who runs that house is Jon Brown," Alex said.

She showed them all a picture of Brown's mug shot.

"Jon Brown is a bad guy," Alex explained. He was a gang banger who migrated to Anchorage, Alaska, with others from his crew. They got into the drug and prostitution trade and were aggressive and violent. Brown has risen to the point where he went independent of his gang and ran his own show. He was smart and a tough customer, seemingly unafraid of the police, and willing to graduate to hyper-violence at the drop of a hat.

Koots was a very large bar and dance club. There was a normal looking bar at the entrance. There were three large separate clubs off the small bar in the front. Those three separate areas had their own stages for live music and dance floors, with tables spread around the floor. What had once been a smallish bar for working men had now become a large gathering place for people of all stripes, but especially young people looking to meet the opposite sex. Some called it a meat market. It had become something of a tourist attraction in the summer.

Several people died in or around the large bar, more than one from violent fights. The bouncers at the bar were big brawlers who earned the well-deserved reputation of inflicting punishment on troublemakers. At least one man had died at the hands of the bouncers. The story was that they would handcuff folks who were causing problems to the log hitching post in front of the bar to wait for the cops to show up.

Alex decided that Stanley and Lilly would enter first and get a table. "We are here to look for Mary Frank, not get drunk or anything. This is recon work, so let's get to it," she said.

Lilly and Stanley made their way around to one of the sections of the club away from the front. They got a table and sat down to watch the dance floor and look for Mary Frank.

Alex and Snow ordered two bottled beers, and Alex dropped a twenty for the bartender who gave a nod of appreciation for the generous tip.

Much to Alex's surprise, Jon Brown appeared from the door leading to the back dance floor and bar that Stanley and Lilly went into. He was flanked by two hulking White men.

Brown was a large Black man, over six foot two and was probably 220 pounds or so. He had on a large overcoat that hung loosely over his large frame. Snow noticed Brown touch or feel a spot on the outside of his coat, most likely a gun. The man had quick attentive eyes and scanned the room as he entered. He glanced toward Alex and Snow, changed directions, and immediately made his way toward them.

"Detective Ramos, by favorite cop bitch! You're looking fine. If you wanna ditch this boy of yours, you can come with me. I'll give you something you can't get with this boy," Brown scoffed with a large smile.

Snow had dealt with tough guys before. In his mind, you had to show immediately that he was unafraid. *Go on the offensive.* He immediately made his play.

Snow stood and squared off in front of Brown. But before he could even utter a word, one of Jon's men grabbed Snow by the arm hard and snarled at him to back off. Snow expected something like this from Jon Brown's muscle, so he was ready for it. *Go for it*, he thought to himself, hard and fast.

Snow slipped the grip and gave the man a hard shot with his right hand to the solar plexus. The move stunned the large man and he slumped back a few steps and bent over. He looked surprised by Snow's move—it's suddenness. These two guys were likely used to people being frightened or backing down. This was different.

The second man waited a couple seconds, then came in hard and took a wild swing at Snow, but Snow ducked and easily slipped behind the man. He slipped his foot around the man's lower leg and tripped the man forward while putting all his weight on the man as he fell forward. The thug hit the bar hard on his chest and went down to his knees.

The first guy had recovered a bit and said, "Gonna teach you a lesson, you little fucker!" He moved in clumsily and took a looping swing with his right. Snow blocked the punch, then landed a crisp left-right combo to the hulk's jaw, and the thug went down like a sack of potatoes.

The other guy stood and rushed Snow who then gave him a furious upper cut to the stomach that doubled him over. When he recovered enough to straighten up, Snow simply gave him a neat one-two to the chops and dropped him like a bad habit.

The whole thing lasted a minute or two, and the two men were on the ground groaning and bleeding into the sawdust. Brown had backed up a few steps, still smirking. But he was looking a little less cocky.

The bar bouncers charged in, but Alex intercepted them, flashing her badge in her hand.

"I got this boys, nothing to worry about," she said to the bouncers.

"I don't think you know who I am," Jon Brown said to Snow, as Alex was dealing with the bouncers.

"You're the guy who's gonna apologize to my friend or you'll be picking your teeth out of the sawdust, friend," Snow said. "Go ahead, why don't you."

"What, apologize?" Job Brown scoffed.

"Go for your piece," Snow dared. "You keep checking it. Go for it so I can take it off you and shove it up your ass."

The two defeated thugs slowly rose to their feet.

"Tell your boys to stay put or they will get hurt this time," Snow mocked.

"Alex, I don't think your friend here knows who I am. Maybe you can talk some sense into him," Brown said while glaring at Snow.

"He knows exactly who you are. You're the banger from Toledo who is up here pimping underage girls," Alex said to Brown. "The guy I am gonna put in jail."

Brown decided to cut his losses.

"I think you have me confused with someone else. Let's go, guys, let's get out of this shit hole," Jon Brown said as he moved to the exit trailed by his limping boys. He turned back and made a signal to Snow with his finger, like he was pointing a gun. Snow did not respond to the final taunt from Jon Brown.

"What in the hell was that, Snow? Jeezus H Christ!" Alex said, like she was mad, but with a smirk.

"I'll take that beer now!" Snow said. He grabbed the bottle of Alaskan Amber off the bar and took a long pull.

CHAPTER 10
THE TAKEDOWN

After checking out the various sections within Chilkoot Charlie's, Lilly and Stanley Beans joined the others in the front bar. They all went to a more private booth but were still in the main front bar section of the giant club.

Alex clued them in on what happened with Jon Brown.

Lilly was clearly upset at Snow for fighting with the men.

"Why did you need to fight them, Brady?" she asked, exasperated.

"They are used to bullying people, and I can't stand that," he said. "Brown is exploiting young girls like Mary Frank and turning them into prostitutes. That makes me angry," he said softly.

"Yes, but you could've gotten hurt, or worse," she scolded.

She turned to Snow and looked into his eyes. "I don't want to lose you," she said.

Alex and Stanley were both studying their beers, listening.

"I am sorry, Lilly. I don't usually do stuff like that, you know. But they were messing with us," Snow said, looking back as her and picking up her hand off the table.

Lilly picked up his right hand and saw that it was red and swollen. "You need to put some ice on this," she said, the nurse in her coming out. "I just don't want you starting any fights, Brady."

Alex and Stanley exchanged a glance and shrugged at the use of Snow's first name.

"If it makes you feel any better, Lilly, Snow did not start the fight. He simply finished it. It looks like he can handle himself pretty good, Lilly. I mean your *novio* put those two big guys down slicker than snot. I was pretty sure he was going to take on Jon Brown too at that point. Though I don't think Brown would go down that easy, and I am sure he was packing. He's always packing. But Snow had that certain look in his eyes, like he was going all in. I've seen that look before," Detective Ramos said.

"And frankly, I was impressed, he did a good job," Alex said taking a sip of her beer.

"We need to get into Jon Brown's house," she said. "I have been working on Jon Brown for some time and have a lot of information I can use. I have a pretty good case built up, but I have an idea we could do something together that would help you find Mary Frank, and help me put him behind bars," she said.

"Eee, I am up for it," Stanley said. "I could go in his place like a customer, you know. They'll let me look at the girls, and I will see if I spot Mary," he said.

"Yeah, I thought of that. But now I have a different idea," Alex said. "But it's asking a lot of you, Lilly." Alex laid out the contours of her plan.

"I don't like it," Snow said.

"I can do it. I want to do it," Lilly said.

"Lilly, I know you are mad at me, but please don't do this," Snow pleaded.

"I am mad at you. But that's not what this is about. I want to do this for the same reasons you fought those guys. It's about the girls like Mary who are being used and abused. I want to help them. And put that guy, Jon Brown, in jail, or at least stop him from what he is doing to them."

"You can help, too, Stanley," Alex said. And so, the plan was initiated.

■ ■ ■

Snow lay in bed that night with Lilly. He was feeling down. The fight had happened in a blink of an eye, but Lilly was right; he did not need to go there. He felt bad, because he made her feel bad. In some ways, he was not used to having another person to worry about. He was used to being alone in the village, and any action he took that could come back to bite him. But now, he had Lilly to consider, and the burden lay heavy upon him.

Snow thought about the big caribou herd he saw at Togiak and it brought him some peace. Copious amounts of frisky calves, more than his eyes could count, frolicking about.

Village life had grown on him, and he longed to return to the slower, more personal pace of life in the bush. It had made him sad to see one of his own, Bill Tuzzy, in the homeless camp.

"I just want to find Mary and go home," Lilly said.

"Me too!" he said.

"Best time of the day," he said to her and snuggled up to her.

"This bed is bad," she said. "Hey, your feet are cold!"

They squirmed around a bit, then relaxed comfortable in their own world, a cocoon filled with love. This was their ritual and made them both feel better.

"Maybe we should get married," Snow whispered.

"Maybe, but I don't think anybody has asked me that question yet," she responded. He smiled and kissed her on the lips. They fell asleep with the drone of Stanley Beans snoring in the living room.

■ ■ ■

Lilly and Stanley went into Avenue Bar, arriving late in the evening. Alex had told them that the girls were usually recruited late when they were intoxicated or looking for a place to party.

Snow was outside in his battered rental car. Lilly was wearing a wire set up by Alex who was monitoring it closely. Snow was in touch with Alex who was in her own vehicle in the Spenard area, where, if they were successful, they would end up.

The Avenue was a long but narrow bar and was full. Several people milled about outside the bar, some smoking, others just hanging out. A couple cabs were parked nearby, ready to give rides to revelers from this bar or others nearby within walking distance. Snow hated the fact that he did not know what was happening inside the bar and was tempted to peek. But he knew that was a bad idea considering that several of Jon Brown's people were inside, including Red, the guy he had put down at Chilkoot Charlie's.

Lilly was standing at the bar talking to Red.

"What happened to your eye?" she asked Red, pointing to his swollen left eye.

"I got sucker punched by some pussy in Koots, but I put him away," Red bragged. Lilly smiled and he took it as a flirtation.

"You want another beer, Lilly?" Red asked, but instead of waiting for an answer, he waved the bartender over. Lilly gave him her real name. Alex had advised to stick to the truth as much as possible, so she did not have to try to keep her story straight.

"I am already pretty high," she said to Red.

"Here, take this, it will help," he offered her a pill.

"It's B vitamins. It will help you from getting too high and will make it so you don't have a hangover," he lied. He had done this same thing many times and was convincing. The pill was the opioid oxycodone, a powerful, addictive narcotic used for people in severe pain. There was a black market for oxy and other pain killers.

"It's okay. I take them all the time; they really help," Red said and popped a similar looking tic tac candy into his mouth. "See, no big deal."

Lilly took the white pill from Red and feigned putting the pill in her mouth when in fact she palmed the pill. She took a drink of beer to simulate washing down the meds. She had practiced this earlier in the day. Red was a bit tipsy and not watching closely.

"Thanks, Red, you're nice," Lilly said and gave him a little smile before looking away.

"You got a place to stay, Lilly?" Red said. He wanted to get this over with and thought he would rather get her out of here before the oxy took hold.

"I do have a place to crash, but I don't like it very much," Lilly said.

"I got a place we can go party if you want. And a place you can crash for the night, too," Red offered.

"I don't know, Red, we just met," Lilly said. *Gotta make him work a bit*, Alex had told her, so he doesn't get suspicious.

But Red wasn't suspicious. Lilly seemed like the typical village girls he met, very naïve and gullible. Trusting, even.

"It's not like that, Lilly. I just meant we can go someplace and have some fun. I know of an after party and people always crash there. It's not my place. I can get you home if you don't want to stay there."

Lilly looked over where Stanley was sitting, hanging out with some people he seemed to know. Stanley seemed to know people everywhere he went.

"Don't worry about your friend; we can come back and get him, too," Red said, noticing Lilly looking to Stanley.

"Okay, maybe for a little while," Lilly said.

Red was pleased by this. *Now we can get this over with so I can get down to some serious drinking,* he thought. He also needed to get back in Jon Brown's good graces, who had been pissed off by him getting beat up at Koots. He did not want to lose his gravy train. He made good money, usually easy working for Brown. The side benefits were plentiful—sex, drugs, and alcohol.

"Great, let's go check it out," Red said, grabbed her by the hand, and led her out of the bar.

They're on the move, Alex texted Snow.

Copy.

Snow saw Lilly and Red exit the Avenue and climb into a yellow cab. Red had a deal with a couple of the cab drivers, so this was normal. They took off heading east, then took a right on C Street towards midtown.

Chief Snow waited for Stanley to come out, which he did right behind Lilly. He jumped in the front seat, and they followed the cab at a distance. There was little traffic. Snow had an idea of where they were headed but was consumed with worry about Lilly, especially if Red or Jon Brown discovered she was wearing a wire. He was pretty sure they would make her disappear or hurt her in such a way that she'd forever regret working with the cops.

"Red has a bad black eye, Chief," Stanley said with delight. "Eee, you got him pretty good!"

Snow was lost in thought and did not respond.

Snow watched the cab pull into a small parking lot behind the house that had a small sign on it that said, *Dating Service and Massage Parlor.* The tattered frame building looked like it had been converted into a whore house. Most of the business it received was generated by word of mouth from people like cab drivers. They also had a social media presence. The sign was simply for potential customers or Johns to know they had the right place.

Snow parked on the street about a block away, but in position to watch the door. He had a small set of binoculars he got from Alex. He took down the license plate of the vehicles in the lot and texted them to Alex. Busy work, but something to do, and it had a purpose.

S car is there, Alex texted back. Snow felt a rush of adrenaline. *S* was cop shorthand for suspect, meaning Jon Brown in this case. At least one of his cars was there. *Good,* he texted back. He added, *Let me know when 2 go. Ready.*

"Okay, Stanley. Things are hot now. I'm gonna get closer to the house. If I take off running toward it, you stay put until the smoke clears, okay?" Snow said.

"Eee, copy that," Stanley said and lit a smoke.

Snow hid behind a car parked near the door, staying in the shadows. He waited and waited. It was starting to drive Snow crazy. Part of police work was the waiting, for sure, but this was a different type of anxiety because of Lilly.

Inside the house, things were happening.

"Want to make some money?" Brown asked Lilly. "You can make some good money, if you want. All you have to do is hang out for a while with a guy. It's easy."

"I don't know," Lilly said. "What do I have to do?"

Jon Brown did not like the feeling he was getting. He could not put his finger on it, but he trusted his gut. He was like a cop in that way. Something was wrong about Lilly; he could feel it.

"Let me see your phone," Jon Brown demanded.

Lilly held it up and Brown reached for it, but Lilly pulled it back.

"I just want to see it,'" Brown said.

"No," Lilly responded.

I knew it! Brown backhanded her across the face, hard enough to knock Lilly down. "Bitch," he said and picked her phone up off the floor where she had dropped it.

Lilly recovered and stood. She was rubbing her face and had a trickle of blood coming from the corner of her mouth. She said, "I'm kinda hungry, do you have any pizza?"

This was the code word if she was in trouble and needed help. But Alex did not hear her say the word, because Brown had quickly disabled the phone.

"I wanna see what you got, you little bitch," Brown snarled.

Jon Brown grabbed Lilly and ripped her blouse down the middle, exposing her bra. Somehow, he had not ripped that too. She tried to run, but Brown grabbed her and threw her to the floor.

Phone off, Alex texted Snow.

Just then, he thought he heard someone scream "PIZZA!" from inside the house. *Lilly!*

Jon Brown was on top of Lilly.

Gotta sample the goods, he thought, *make this little bitch pay for whatever she's up to.*

"You a feisty little squaw," Brown muttered. "You some kinda undercover snitch?"

Lilly was strong and was squirming under John Brown, trying to free herself. She screamed "PIZZA" again at the top of her lungs.

"Pizza? What kind of nut job are you?" Jon Brown mocked.

Lilly could do little to slow him down as he ripped her bra off by grabbing it. Lilly screamed and covered her breasts. But Brown moved down her black jeans, clawing at them. Lilly had to uncover herself to try and keep her pants on. Suddenly, she stuck her thumb in Brown's eye, but he moved his head and backhanded her again, hard.

Snow crashed through the front door and blew right past Red. He saw Brown on top of Lilly and jumped toward them. He punched at Jon Brown's head but did not get full purchase.

Red came up and grabbed from behind. Snow wheeled and threw a furious flurry of punches that put Red back on the ground in about ten seconds flat, just as he did the night before.

Jon Brown pulled his gun out of his paddle holster in his belt, and started to raise it, but Snow was back on him. The chief grabbed the gun and pulled it toward his chest. The gun discharged into the ceiling. There was smoke and the smell of cordite in the air. Snow wrenched the gun down, and it flew away out of Brown's hand, away from Snow.

"YOU!" Brown said. I am going to enjoy this, you little fucker!" Brown hollered.

"Me too!" Snow responded, and the fight was on.

Lilly scrambled to get the gun, one hand holding her ripped blouse. With the other, she grabbed the gun. She was ready to shoot Brown; in her mind, she wanted to kill him. She grabbed the gun and looked up to see Mary Frank looking down at her.

"Mary! We are here to save you!" Lilly said.

"Lilly? Lilly!" Mary said and started to cry.

Brown rushed at Snow and drove him into a wall, busting up an end table and crashing into a cheap display as they smashed into the wall. Snow had landed a heavy straight right to Brown's nose as he came in, but it didn't have any effect in stopping him.

They crashed into the wall, and Snow was under Brown, but only for a moment. He pivoted out as he had done a thousand times when he was a wrestler. They both were up, and Brown waded back in, his nose broken and bleeding.

Snow landed a left and right before Brown was on him again. He used a wrestling move to slip behind Brown. He locked his hands in the front, around Brown's waist. He then picked him up with all his might and slammed him to the floor with as much force as possible, using his weight to try and maximize the pain.

The move seemed to stun Jon Brown for a second, and that was all Snow needed. He slipped his right arm around Brown's neck and put him in a choke hold. Brown struggled to get to his feet, and Snow simply put his legs around Brown's waist and locked them up around his middle. Brown's motion had simply tightened Snow's hold around his neck.

Brown was weakening and starting to fade. The house had been pandemonium for the past few minutes. In the door came Detective Ramos and two more uniforms. Alex had her gun drawn, pointed at Brown who was facing her. He dropped to his knees, fading fast as he futilely clawed Snow's arm.

"Clear the house!" Alex shouted, and the two uniformed cops immediately began searching the house for other threats. They cuffed Red just as Alex pulled a pair of handcuffs from her back pocket and slid them on the floor over to Snow.

"Let loose, Snow. Cuff him. I got him," she said with her gun pointed at Brown.

Snow let loose and pushed Brown forward to a prone position. Brown gasped for air as Snow quickly put cuffs on his hands behind his back. He was exhausted and his hands and fingers were shaking.

"Clear! Clear!" the two uniforms announced as they came back into the main room where Alex was holstering her sidearm.

"Okay, then. We got'm Snow," she said.

"What took you so long?" Snow said tiredly. The left corner of his mouth went up in what was all he could muster for a smile.

Alex smiled a brilliant smile back at Snow and choked out a half laugh.

■ ■ ■

It took a couple days for things to kind of get cleared up. Alex and her crew took statements from all people involved. She had enough to put Jon Brown away for a good long time. But she wanted him in cement shoes. But what she really wanted was to roll up his operation.

Lilly and Mary Frank had been taken to Providence Medical Center to get checked out. Lilly had demanded that they share a room, and this had been done, with Alex's help. Lilly was okay but shaken; she was tough and recovered quickly. Mary was coming out of a long drug induced nightmare; it would take longer for her to recover.

When Alex came to interview Mary Frank, she broke down and said she would only talk to Lilly. As Lilly was talking to Mary, Snow came in the hospital room that had been set up for the interview.

Mary Frank got up and came to him and gave him a long hug, sobbing.

"You guys came for me!" she said through tears.

"Lilly was the one. She set all this up. But really, the whole village was worried about you. They sent us, Lilly, Stanley, and me, to find you. They want you to come home," Snow said close to tears himself. He looked at Lilly over Mary's shoulder. They shared a long look at each other. "They will take care of you. You are safe now."

Stanley came into the room, and they had a tiny Togiak reunion. Mary Frank laughed as Stanley told her some news about home.

Mary Frank ended up giving compelling testimony that would cement a case of trafficking against Jon Brown.

It was over, Snow thought. But it was not.

CHAPTER 11
POOK

James Pook got out of jail on bail a few days after he had been arrested and charged for shooting up the Round House, the same night Lilly shot him in the femur with the 22. He had gotten an infection, which was a fine excuse for the jail and the court to kick Pook loose.

Pook rubbed his thigh and grimaced.

"Best damn infection I ever got," he said to no one in particular. He was sitting in his favorite chair, watching *The Price is Right* on TV. He got used to watching the show while he was in jail and continued the routine when he got home. It gave him a sense of structure and routine. That was one thing about jail that he missed, the structure. He had done several stretches in jail, the longest about two years. Life revolved around mealtimes and TV shows. He knew many of the inmates, and he had some stature in the jail system.

Pook was back in his home in Togiak. The home was in a row of what people referred to as HUD houses. They were all the same design and layout, until, over time, they became more personalized. Some were painted differently, and others had added on a lean-to or something else that made them distinctive. Pook's house was light yellow. He and his cousin JJ had built a larger cunny chuck, or arctic entry, to the side of the house. It was a place to put boots and coats, and sometimes there would be a caribou quarter hanging there. Several long guns were also leaning in one corner of the cunny chuck. The inside of the house had deteriorated in the years since it had been built, to the point where it was a bit seedy. Still, in all, it was a comfortable home for him and his battered wife, Nancy. It was warm and cozy, his sanctuary.

They had one son, but the boy had some serious mental health issues, and he decided it was better that he lived with his Akka, or grandmother. It was common for kids to live with grandparents or cousins in the village. Often it was because of drinking or domestic violence in the parent's home. In this instance, it was a good thing for everyone. Good for the child not to be around his abusive and violent father, and good for Pook who did not appreciate his son's issues.

After the shooting, he was under strict court ordered conditions of release not to drink alcohol or possess firearms, among other restrictions. He took a swig of Rich and Rare, R and R whiskey, and water and grimaced. He picked up his shotgun and checked the action, and generally looked it over before setting it down.

Pook understood what the court conditions were about. They were intended to keep people on a leash. They were meant for other people, though, but not him. He also understood that the conditions of release were toothless. The jails were too full, and they were not going to yank him back on a chicken shit release violation. Besides, that little peckerwood Snow was out of town, and he knew none of the other cops had the sand to arrest him on a violation of release.

Pook was unemployed and, in fact, worked only sporadically in his life. There were not many jobs in the village anyway, and unemployment was extremely high. Like many people, he lived a more subsistence lifestyle. He hunted and fished for the bulk of their food. Pook was a fair hunter and they usually had plenty of meat. They survived largely on the food he could provide off the land. And on government checks they got from one source or another. The checks allowed him to buy food, weed, and alcohol. He would bootleg alcohol at times, the idea being to supplement their meager income. But as was often the case with bootleggers or dealers, he was his own best customer.

"Nancy! Bring me something to eat!" he hollered at his wife. "I'm cleaning my gun."

Pook also had a handgun on the end table next to him, mostly just to admire it. He rarely cleaned it. The gun was not really his anyway. He had taken it from his nephew. They had been sitting having a drink, both a bit high at that time. His nephew was talking about his new gun, and Pook had asked to see it. The nephew had proudly handed it over for Pook to examine.

"I like this. It's sweet," Pook had said to his nephew. It became apparent to the nephew that Pook was not giving it back.

"Hey, can I get that back now?" the nephew asked after some time. It was obvious to Pook that the nephew was scared. He had a fine-tuned sensibility at gauging fear in others. He could tell when people were intimidated by him, almost as if he could smell it on them.

"I'm gonna borrow it," Pook said. The nephew looked relieved. And that was that. He never gave it back.

Pook picked up the gun and looked it over. It was a beauty. Blued Colt 45 with walnut grips. He loved to hold it, and to carry it. It felt so solid and well-made and added to his overall sense of power.

Pook was a hard case. He was not born evil but had become that way over the years. Any redeeming qualities he may have had were long gone. Smothered by the abuse he had suffered at the hands of his father and uncle, both physical and sexual. As a method of coping with the scars and stain on his soul from the abuse, he drank. A lot.

The booze made him feel a bit human at times. Even made him feel good, though never quite happy. The problem was that it could also make him mean. Real mean.

Nancy came in and set a plate on the table next to him with eggs and spam on it.

"What took you so long?!" he scolded as she scurried back to the kitchen. *Got to keep them in line,* he thought.

He had learned not to let up, not to give her any space. Nancy was damaged by the incessant barrage of physical and emotional abuse. She was once a slender and attractive woman but was now a shadow of that person. He did not care or even give a thought to her needs, except as it pertained to him.

Pook had once made the mistake of being nice to Nancy. It had happened in a weak moment when he was feeling generous. It became clear to him that time that even one random act of kindness would lead to expectations by Nancy of more. He realized his mistake and had to rectify the situation by giving her a savage beating. Since that time, he would never show her the least bit of respect or kindness. There was no love and the sex had ceased long ago. As long as she could continue to make him food and clean up the house, she had a purpose. And of course, she got checks, too.

Pook got up and stretched. He needed to get out of the house and get some fresh air. There were things he had really missed in jail—the freedom to go outside and ride his four-wheeler. And hunting.

Pook was aware, he had heard through the small-town grapevine, that Chief Snow and his little band of idiots had gone to Anchorage to search for Mary Frank. That was good and bad. It was good because, with Snow out of town, he had been free to bring home alcohol with little concern. In fact, he had gone directly from jail to the liquor store and grabbed a case of whiskey. He would sell a few bottles to pay for it and keep the rest for himself.

The bad part was that he was involved in Mary Frank's disappearance in Anchorage.

■ ■ ■

Pook had gotten to know Red, who worked for Jon Brown, when he had been in Anchorage previously. Red had offered him money, drugs, or booze, if he could send him young women from the village to Anchorage. That young girl, Mary Frank, the one his wife had mentioned, would fit the bill. She was young and naïve, good looking, and her family was a mess.

Pook went home and pressed his Nancy about Mary Frank.

"She's pretty and real social and wants to get out of Anchorage," Nancy said. "The village guys are all over her."

"Then go get her," James Pook ordered. "Red needs girls for his prostitution ring in Anchorage. We can make a nice chunk of change delivering a cutey like her. Get it done . . . or else."

Nancy didn't want to sell the sweet girl into prostitution. But she knew if she failed, her husband would beat her. So, she reached out to Mary Frank and the two met over a couple of beers.

"Look, sweetie. There's an opportunity that me and James heard about in Anchorage. There are some clubs there that need bartenders and waitresses and hostesses. They pay pretty well and even set you up with a place to stay. You could have fun meeting new people and make some decent money while you're at it."

"I'm not finished with school yet," Mary Frank said. "And how would I get to Anchorage?"

"Come on, Mary. You don't need a high school diploma to make decent money in Anchorage. You're just wasting your time. I never finished school and I'm doing okay. And as far as getting down there, it wouldn't cost you a thing. It would be all arranged."

■ ■ ■

Pook never really tracked what happened to Mary Frank once she hit the big town. But he was somewhat pleased when he heard she was missing. That meant things had worked out on Red's end. Which meant that he could ask for additional money, or at the very least would keep the door open for sending another girl to Anchorage. It appeared as though he would collect more on Mary.

Pook was worried about Snow and the others looking for her. It was kind of a vague worry; there were a lot of unknowns. But Snow kept mucking up his life. That was his real issue. *Snow.* He had given a lot of thought about him. He was a problem that needed to go away. He thought that Snow would leave the village after a while, because most of the cops and teachers who came in from outside lasted only a short time and left. Most simply couldn't handle village life and all it entailed. When Snow arrested him the first time, he had been very surprised. Pook was used to people being scared of him, even the piss-poor cops the village usually hired. He could simply intimidate them or scare them out of town. But it had been clear that day after they had gotten into a ground fight, and Snow had actually bested him, that this cop was different. He was not scared or intimidated.

Pook's next step had been to really try and put the fear of God into Snow and his little girlfriend Lilly. He figured if Lilly got frightened enough, she would want to leave, and likely Snow would go as well. That was why he went to Snow's place, the Round House, and shot it up that night. Even though he was pretty high that night, he had still given it some considerable thought. It just so happened that he often acted when he had some booze in him. The big surprise was that little bitch Lilly. He never expected her to interfere—let alone to shoot him.

Now he was thinking about what to do next.

Pook had his Colt 45 in the pocket of his coat; he had stowed the shotgun in the cunny chuck or entryway of his house as he limped out.

It was a fine spring day; the air was fresh and clean. Snow fell but the temperature was warm—at least for this part of the world.

Pook drove around the village on his four-wheeler lost in thought. He was not a deep thinker by any means. Most everything he thought about pertained directly to him and his needs. In that way, he was a narcissist. And a sociopath. He would do anything to meet his needs. If there was potential for him to get hurt or end up in jail, well, that was a consideration for sure. But he gave no thought about others needs or even if they got hurt.

Pook drove to the beach by the Round House. He wondered about going inside, with Snow out of town. He smiled when he saw that the window of the front door was still boarded up. He thought about going in and trashing the place. Or burning it down. But it seemed like too much work at the moment, and he drove past.

Pook pulled up in front of the AC Store and walked in. He needed a pack of smokes. The store was impressive. It had been built a few years ago, but still seemed new to Pook. It had wide aisles and was clean. They stocked a bit of everything, including clothing, hardware, and just about anything needed in the village. The one thing they did not have much of was fresh produce. It was logistically difficult to get fresh fruit and vegetables into the village and was not practical to keep it in stock.

Pook wandered around a bit and looked at items on the shelves. It was a very village thing to do. After some time, he got his Marlboros and continued his ride. He had missed smoking in jail, that was for sure.

He drove out to the gravel airport and continued past, heading south along the coast. He drove all the way to the end of the road and up a high riverbank that overlooked Togiak Bay. He sat on his machine and smoked, then headed back into town. Instead of going home, though, he took the one road that went west. There was a new part of the town that was being gradually built up over the years. It was about a mile inland and ran parallel to the main village. The plan was to move the entire village up there eventually. Like many villages in Alaska, Togiak was built right on the water. That left the town susceptible to floods and storms. And the tides and increasing number of storms were eating away the bank that the town was built on. It only made sense to move the town to higher ground at some point.

He drove west toward the gentle hills of the new development. Instead of turning south to drive the one road in that direction where there was a small row of new houses, he took a well-worn trail that continued into the hills east of town.

He came to an overlook and stopped his four-wheeler. He looked east and saw caribou in the distance grazing in the valley between two hills, a small herd of maybe a couple hundred caribou or so, a splinter group of the main herd. He scoped the herd with his binoculars.

After a bit, he heard a four-wheeler coming his way. His cousin JJ pulled up beside him and killed his engine.

Pook said, "Took you long enough! I was thinking of drinking the jug myself."

JJ smiled and lifted his leg over the tank, getting off the four-wheeler to stretch.

"How much?" he asked.

"Three hundred," Pook said.

"I only got two-fifty. I can pay you the rest when I get my check," JJ said. He sauntered over to Pook and held the money out in his right hand.

Pook looked over his shoulder on the right, and then the left. Habit. He pulled a plastic jug of R and R out of the interior pocket of his tan Carhart jacket. He unscrewed the top and took a swig, then handed it to JJ who took a short swig before he put the pint bottle into the inside pocket of his jacket. He returned to sit on his four-wheeler.

They both watched the caribou for some time, enjoying the pleasant warmth of the alcohol.

"You see that?" JJ pointed south away from the caribou. "Wolf, I think."

Pook picked up his field glasses from the fuel tank where he had set them. He scanned the area and indeed spotted a wolf trotting away toward the herd, where it suddenly stopped and drooped to the ground.

"Good eye!" Pook said to JJ. It was a rare thing to spot a wolf, and he felt pleased at the sight.

"Wanna go hunt?" JJ asked after a time.

"Nah, not today. Gonna drink some, and besides, my leg is still fucked up," Pook said. "But we need to go sometime while they are close."

"That Lilly! She's something, ain't she? I wouldn't mind a piece of that. She's smoking hot, man!" JJ said, thinking about Lilly when Pook mentioned his leg.

Pook slowly shook his head. "She needs to be taught a lesson. But the bitch is cute."

"She shouldn't be with no cop," JJ scowled. "She's a good nurse too. She took care of my kid when he got sick. Fixed him up real good."

"Gotta do something about the snowflake she is with. That fucking cop. He is a real pain in my ass. He needs to go hunting," said Pook, referring to the idea of two people going out to hunt, and only one coming back. Same thing with fishing. A good number of people died in hunting or fishing *accidents*.

"Give me another pull, would you?"

JJ retrieved the bottle and took a pull, then put the cover on and tossed it to Pook who caught it easily. After a minute, he took another pull off the bottle and tossed it back to JJ.

Pook had a sudden thought. An idea.

"I think I might need your help," Pook said to JJ.

CHAPTER 12
THE BATTLE OF SITKA

With Mary now safe, Chief Snow said he would meet Lilly and Stanley back at the village. He wanted to return to Sitka to spend more time with his mother and learn about his Tribal roots.

Back at Lanny's house, they moved back to the small room where they had talked the first night Snow came to town. Snow looked around the room while Lanny used the bathroom.

Snow observed the various Tribal items around the room. He had seen plenty in the past, but he looked at them now through different eyes, as something he was connected to, something he now knew was part of his very own heritage. It was hard for him to say exactly what the feeling was, but he thought it might be pride.

Snow picked up the spruce root hat that Lanny had left on the coffee table. He examined it closely, eyeing at the workmanship and wondering how patient someone had to be to weave the reeds in such a way. After a minute or so, he tried the hat on, and it fit. He quickly took it off, feeling a bit like he was doing something wrong.

He wandered over to the bookshelf and looked at the books

and other items arrayed there. He picked up a small baleen box and examined it closely. Again, he was struck by the craftsmanship in the highly detailed little box. He also looked at a similar sized bentwood box, which had the distinct aroma of cedarwood, a smell recalled from his adopted mother's cedar chest, a smell he always enjoyed, bringing him a touch of pleasant nostalgia from his childhood.

Lanny came in the room and lit an incense stick. She noticed the spruce root hat, picked it up, and said to Snow, "You should try this on, see if it fits you."

Snow smiled and said, "Already did, I am ashamed to say. It actually fits me pretty good."

"You know what, I would have liked to see you in your police uniform. Just to see you as others see you," Lanny said.

The two took to their seats.

"So, what happens to Katlian and the Kiksadi, Lanny?" Snow asked.

"Okay, I will finish the story. My, my, you are as impatient as Katlian," she said with a smile.

As Lanny began to tell her story, Snow noticed a shape in the dark doorway off to his left.

"Kee!" Snow exclaimed. "Good to almost see you! How did you get here? You just seemed to materialize like a ship coming out of the fog," Snow exuded as Kee took her usual position in the darkened doorway.

"It's good to see you smile!" he said.

Kee shook her rattle once. It seemed to be a recognition to what Snow said to her, but it was not clear at all.

"Hello, Kee, good to see you again," Lanny said. Kee settled into the darkness and Snow thought she may be smiling.

Lanny resumed her story, picking up exactly where she had left off days before.

■ ■ ■

The Russians had used several smaller boats to tow the large ship, Neva, into place during the night. The smaller boats all had oars and men to row them. The Tlingit were aware of the movement but did not respond in force to try and stop them. The Neva was now in position to begin hammering the fort with her cannons.

But that did not happen. Instead, the Russians launched what they hoped would be a surprise and overwhelming attack against the Tlingit. Lord Baranof himself was leading the attack.

It was not a surprise to Katlian. He had been aware when he met with Captain Lisianski that the captain may be feeding him false information. When the Neva began to position itself directly in front of the fort, he knew that it could open fire with cannons, but that it could also be an operational base for an attack against the fort. He was prepared and had made plans for either. In fact, it was the latter.

Additional Russian battle ships had entered the bay, but Neva was the closest to the shore and in position to directly fire at the Tlingit stronghold.

"This is what I am talking about," Snow interrupted. Lanny looked up at him with mild annoyance, but also with a smile, as if amused by a rambunctious child.

"I mean, Katlian was a very tactical, strategic leader, it seems to me," Snow said. "He was not tricked or intimidated by the Russian's obvious superiority in firepower and technology. I mean, the warships, you would think Katlian would have been a bit intimidated. But instead, he had various contingencies. I mean, he is far from an adrenaline junkie warrior. I am impressed by Katlian."

"You are about to become more impressed," Lanny said, foreshadowing the next sequence of her story. "Now, stop interrupting!" she said with mock anger.

"Sorry, Mother," Snow responded sarcastically.

Kee shook her rattle.

After the meeting with Lisianski, Katlian met with the Tribal leaders.

"We do not have the men we need to fend off a major attack!" Stoon had counseled the group. Some heads nodded, and some sounds of agreement were heard.

Much to Katlian and the group's surprise, Nami spoke.

"I can fight. The women can fight too!" she said quietly but in a voice that all could hear.

She went to the wall and grabbed a spear and held it in her hands for emphasis. A low murmur went through the council and others in attendance at the war council meeting being held in one of the longhouses inside the fort.

"No. Women do not fight in our battles. It has not been done before; it is not our way," Stoon commented with authority.

"It is one thing to hold a spear, another to use it in battle," he continued with some irony, since as Shaman he had never fought in battle.

"AIEEEE!" Nami screamed and stabbed the spear with force into one of the logs on the interior of the longhouse. The spear did not lodge in the wood, so she withdrew it and screamed again and stabbed the spear with force again into a log, lower this time. It stuck, and she left it sticking out of the log for all to see.

Nami's action had surprised everyone. They all stood and there was a clamor of voices as they watched her. She also surprised them with her dexterity and strength and her apparent ability to handle the spear. She turned to face them, the spear still stuck in the log, swaying in the firelight behind her. Her hair had come partly free from its binds and was loose and wild. She looked fierce and wild at that moment as she said loudly, "I can fight too!"

The men in the room cheered for her!

"Wow!" What a woman!" Snow whispered in awe, low, almost under his breath. He imagined that Nami was Lilly; it was how he pictured it in his mind. It brought a lump to his throat.

Kee shook her rattle several times in apparent agreement.

Lanny continued, her eyes almost shut, almost in a trance.

The men had been talking at once, but when Katlian spoke in a commanding voice, the other men sat in silence.

"We need warriors! I don't care if they are men, or women, or bears! As long as they can fight!" he said loudly. The men cheered again, more boisterous than before.

Katlian shared his plan for responding to the Russian attack, and it included deployment of women to fight and support the battle.

Later, in private, he gently scolded Nami by saying, "Stoon was right; this is not our way for women to fight."

"No. You were right the first time. Man, woman, or bear, you said as long as they can fight!" she said. She was close to tears.

Katlian saw her emotion and gathered her in an embrace. He kissed her face and her cheeks, then her hair. He held her tight as he whispered, "You are my warrior. I love you with all my heart. I am proud of my wife, Nami the Fierce!" She shook in his arms. "Besides," he continued, "I think poor Stoon shit himself when you screamed and stabbed the wall. It was definitely worth it!" Nami sobbed and laughed.

"I should have told you what I was thinking," she said. "But it happened before I could stop myself. I mean, if I had thought about it beforehand, I would have told you. My Captain!" she said with some heat in her voice.

"I am your husband. And you are my love," Katlian said and kissed Nami on the lips.

■ ■ ■

Katlian watched with interest in the early dawn light. The Russian war ship Neva was close enough that he could clearly see them make their preparations for the attack. They are overconfident, thought Katlian.

Katlian was dressed for battle. He put on his Raven helmet, which was primarily made of wood and surprisingly light. It had protection for the lower part of his face, unlike the other helmet he had worn for the meeting with Lisianski which was more for ceremony and less for protection.

In some ways, this helmet was even more impressive as it was topped with a raven's beak, the symbol of his clan. It was stained dark, almost as dark as a raven's wing. Katlian was a Raven of the Kiksadi clan.

He had his new favorite weapon in his hand, the handheld blacksmith's sledge he had taken with him from the raid at the Russian camp they called Saint Michaels. Nami had painted his face with black diagonal stripes, though they were mostly covered by the helmet.

He wore his protective vest made from lightweight wooden slats but was bare-chested underneath. He liked the freedom of movement this afforded. He was barefoot; again, this was his choice. The soles of his feet were toughened to the point that he could run overtop rocks without an issue. Again, he preferred the freedom of movement over the relative protection of wearing some type of foot covering.

He was wearing a knife at his waist, a long blade that he had traded for some time ago. It was his favorite knife. It originally had a wooden handle, but that had worn out due to his constant use of it. He had replaced the wooden handle with one carved from a deer's antler. In preparation for battle, he had spent time during the night sharpening the blade with a stone. It was sharp.

Katlian had one of his many spears, and a musket with shot and powder was nearby as well. The battle would determine what battle implements he would employ.

As Katlian monitored the Russian activity, he went up and down the inside of the fort, checking on his men who were lined up inside the fort wall facing the water. Most were peering out at the Russian activity between the cracks and logs.

"Check your muskets. Check your gear. Recheck it!" Katlian said as he paced up the line of men who stopped peering out and got busy checking their war gear. He took the time to put his hand on each man as he passed by.

"Don't worry, they are coming," he said. "And we will greet them!"

The Russians were loading two small portable cannons onto the large row boats at the side of the Neva. Aleut warriors in kayaks were hovering about nearby, ready for the order. Men, arms, ammunition, and other items were loaded onto the large row boats. Finally, Baranof came aboard. When he did so, the boat pushed off, and the order was given. Attack the fort.

The numerous small kayaks and Aleut warriors led the way for the other rowboats. Russian soldiers were only in the larger boats. In all, there were over 150 warriors in the Russian battle, now heading for the beach in front of the Tlingit fort. The tide was low and there was a considerable open stretch of beach and rocks in front of the fort. Katlian wondered if they had considered the tide in their battle plan.

"Hold your fire!" Katlian said. He did not want to waste any ammunition, until he was sure they were in range.

The first wave of kayaks was on the beach, but the Aleuts did not immediately charge. They waited for the larger boats to begin to make landfall, so apparently the Russian captains could organize the attack.

"Baranof!" Katlian said as he spotted the Russian Commander in one of the large row boats. So, he was not so frightened after all!

"FIRE!" Katlian shouted.

A thunderous volley was sent at the Russians and Aleuts by the Tlingit warriors, the musket barrels stuck out of cracks between the logs. Several Aleut warriors were hit.

"AGAIN!" Katlian ordered. Gun smoke was wafting through the inside of the fort.

A second volley was sent toward the attackers. Baranof was hit and went down.

A group of young Tlingit's, and some Tlingit women, were loading the muskets for another volley. But Katlian seized the moment; it appeared the attackers were in disarray. He saw them negotiating the mobile cannon out of the boats and onto the beach. He did not want them to start firing those cannons.

"CHARGE!" Katlian cried. He was already halfway out of the fort when he screamed the order. He screamed charge again and led a group of warriors toward the attackers on the beach. His hammer was held high above his head, and he screamed a war cry again. He heard Nami scream behind him in a higher pitch. He didn't want her too close to the front of the attack and picked up his pace.

"CHARGE!" Katlian screamed again but in the direction of the woods adjacent to the fort.

A second group of Tlingit warriors emerged from hiding! He heard their war cries as he then engaged the Russian force from the side in a flanking, or pincer type of move Katlian had planned for the attack. It was his idea to throw another force to roll up their flank and hopefully disorient the Russians.

There was a clatter of noise as the groups met in battle. He heard screams and the clank of spears clashing against muskets or shields. and the sound of muskets being fired. Smoke filled the battle area. A stout Aleut warrior screamed and thrust a spear at him, but he slapped it aside and violently brought his hammer down on the warrior. It hit the warrior's left shoulder and snapped bones as the Aleut let out a cry of pain. Katlian had already began a second swing, and it hit the warrior directly on the head. Blood and bone squirted as the warrior collapsed.

Katlian sought another target in the chaotic melee. He saw a fierce hand-to-hand battle off to his right and stepped in and ended that contest with one thunderous blast from his hammer to the neck of another Aleut warrior that simply crumpled the warrior from the blow.

He heard Nami scream from behind him and spun around. A Russian solider had a musket raised in the air poised to strike down at Katlian. Except the Russian had the bloody point of a spear poking out of his stomach and seemed frozen in place. The soldier's eyes were big with surprise, shock, and pain. Katlian strode forward, the hammer came down, and the Russian soldier's bones made a snap and crackle as the hammer caved in the man's upper chest.

Nami put her foot on his back and forcefully pulled the spear out of the dead soldier's back.

Katlian looked around, a heat seeker looking for a target.

The Russian force was in full disarray and retreating. Baranof had been hit and was already in one of the boats. Several soldiers were trying to muscle the small cannons back into the boats. Aleuts were retreating to their kayaks, some already back in the water, warriors pushing them out, others paddling like mad.

Katlian ran at the men wrestling with the cannons. He gave a war cry, his hammer held high, ready to destroy. He saw an Aleut stand up in a kayak close to shore and fire a musket at him. The Aleut was hit by a bullet and went down, but not before he got the shot off. Katlian got hit with a musket ball, but it hit his protective vest in the chest area, saving him. The concussion slowed him a step, but he quickly recovered and attacked the men working to lift one of the cannons into the boat.

The hammer came down again and again. Two men crumpled into the surf under its devastating blows of the hammer. Others in the boats pushed off the shore with oars, leaving the cannon in the surf. Katlian looked around, back and forth looking for other targets to engage. But the fight had ended as quickly as it had begun. The Russians were in full retreat in their boats, paddling like mad away from the Tlingit.

Katlian gave a huge victory cry with his bloody hammer raised! A cheer went up from his warriors!

They had repulsed the attack by the Russians! Victory!

There were dead and wounded on the beach; some Tlingit were down. But mostly it was Aleut warriors and a handful of Russian soldiers. The two cannons the Russians had meant to use were never fired that day, and were lost to them, abandoned in their retreat. The attack by the Russians had been an utter failure.

In part because their commander, Baranof, had gone down, hit by a musket shot. They were able to get him into a boat and away; it was unclear if the wound was mortal or not.

The Neva opened fire with her cannons to cover the retreat of the soldiers on the beach. Although the shots were wildly long and over their heads, it got the Tlingit's attention and spurred them to move quickly now.

The wounded Tlingit were immediately hauled into the fort. The Russian and Aleut, dead and wounded, were left on the beach. A couple that had been gravely wounded were put out of their misery by the Tlingit warriors. Katlian saw Nami put a spear in the heart of a gravely wounded Aleut warrior laying in the sand and rocks. Mercy killing. Katlian used his knife to cut the throat of one of the mortally wounded Aleut warriors.

The cannons were also left to the tide for now, as the Tlingit's retreated to the safety of their fort Shís'gi Noow.

■ ■ ■

Lanny stopped talking. Tears were streaming down her face. The telling had drained her emotionally.

She stood up, and Snow did as well. He went over and gave Lanny a hug. Kee had left as mysteriously as she had come.

CHAPTER 13
KIKSADI

Chief Snow met his mother the next day and they walked to the Westmark Shee Attica Hotel for an early lunch. It was their last night together before Snow had to return to his village.

Lanny was very curious about her son's adventures in Sitka, especially his encounter with the bear.

"It's so sad they had to kill it," Lanny said. "I mean, I am sure it was necessary. But the truth is, usually the young bears get pushed into town by the bigger males. They are more scared of the big male bears than they are of us. They get drawn into town by the garbage or other things to eat. Dogs, unfortunately. It just makes me sad when they have to kill a young bear like that," Lanny said.

"Yeah, me too. Though I would say, things are different out in the village. A bear that comes near town is a dead bear. Just the way it is out there. They don't want to mess around with a kid getting mauled or something like that," Snow commented.

"That's true. When I was in Barrow, the locals would shoot a polar bear pretty much on sight," Lanny said.

"Didn't know you were up on the North Slope," he said, curious.

"Oh, yeah. I been all over, up north, out west, Anchorage, Fairbanks, working on one thing or another," Lanny said. Then Lanny resumed her story about Katlian.

■ ■ ■

"I don't think we can win a prolonged war with the Russians," Katlian had said to his wife Nami.

They were in their private space in one of the longhouses within the Shís'gi Noow, the Tlingit fort on the mouth of the Indian River.

"This is not what I expected to hear from you, Kut. I thought after the great victory today you would be anxious to engage the Russians, to fight them," Nami said.

"On a personal level, I am. If it was just about me, I would fight them until the end. But I am thinking about the Tribe. We don't have the resources to maintain a long fight against the Russians," Katlian said.

"We are basically out of gunpowder. The Russians appear to have more men and more and bigger arms. Additionally, we have children and Elders here to consider. And food could become an issue at some point as well," Katlian said, thinking out loud.

"Stoon wants to retreat from the battle, so you would have his support, I believe, if we do decide to move to another of our camps and abandon this fort," Nami said, referring to the Shaman Stooncook.

After the battle, the Tlingit had been rejoicing. Even with the Russian warship, Neva firing her cannons at the fort, which for today at least had not done any damage. The drums had been beating throughout the evening, and most were very happy. Even those who lost someone in the battle were pleased that their loved one was lost in such a successful and important battle, repulsing the Russian attack.

Katlian was extremely pleased with the outcome, as his battle plan had worked very well.

The Russians had been overwhelmed. Perhaps they were surprised at the attack. Or maybe it was overconfidence, or poor intelligence. The pincer move was helpful as well and seemed to quickly break the spirit of the attack. And Baranof going down early in the battle was surely a factor. He was not even sure that Baranof was alive.

The next day, the Neva began to shell the fort in earnest. The Russians had done some ranging shots the day before and therefore were able to adjust the range. Now the shelling was hitting the fort. As yet, the fort had held under direct hits. Shot after shot was on target, hitting the walls of the fort, but they all simply bounced off. The Tlingit had moved all people to the outer walls in case the Russians were able to drop shots inside the walls of the fort. But that did not happen, as the Russians continually took aim at the walls of the fort to try and break down the Tlingit palisade.

Later that afternoon, the Russian cannons stopped. It seemed the Russians may be reconsidering their battle plans.

A rowboat approached the shore under a flag of truce.

"Emissary!" was the call, repeated around the inside of the fort.

Katlian and Nami again met the emissary to talk, accompanied by a group of warriors in case it was a trick or trap. As was the case of the previous meeting, it was Lisianski with his wife on the boat sent as emissary, along with a contingent of warriors and soldiers.

The meeting was more direct that the last, with neither side quite as diplomatic and polite. People had died the day before on both sides, and there was a sullenness now, not the bravado of the first meeting.

"Lord Baranof demands the immediate surrender of the Tlingit force," Lisianski said in Russian.

"Where is your Lord? He was hit by a musket ball in your humiliating defeat," Katlian said in Tlingit. *He was blunt but did not say these things in anger or with a raised voice.*

"Your guns cannot hurt Lord Baranof," Lisianski said enigmatically. *The truth was that Baranof had a protective chainmail garment he wore under his outer uniform. Much like Katlian's wooden vest, it saved his life from the bullet. But he had been hurt, cracked ribs and deeply bruised.*

"Not the way it looked to me. I was in the battle, not you. I saw your Lord get hit and fall. I saw your weakling Aleuts have to help him into the boat. This was right before your attacking force was routed, and wisely decided to run away, like frightened seagulls. Thank you for the cannons," Katlian said. *Again, he was blunt but did not speak in anger.*

"Your surrender is the demand. I know you do not have the firepower to withstand an extended siege. You know it too," Lisianski said frankly.

"Your cannon balls do not damage our fort as you can plainly see," Katlian said, waving his left arm toward the fort.

"Nonetheless, we demand your immediate surrender. We await your answer," Lisianski said, ending the talk.

Katlian took the surrender demand to the leadership, and scoffed at it.

"Can't they see their cannons are useless against Shís'gi Noow," one clan leader said.

"They know it," Katlian said.

They talked into the night and a plan was developed. But before they finished up, they sent an emissary to the Neva with a message for the Russians demanding their surrender.

Snow laughed at that and shook his head. "Katlian has some serious stones!" he said. Lanny nodded and continued.

The back and forth between the Russian and the Tlingit continued for two days, with breaks to exchange emissaries with demands. The Russians continued to fire cannons at the Tlingit fort but were unable to breach the walls. No additional major attacks on land were made.

On the third day since the initial attack, Katlian sent word that he wanted to talk of peace. This time, Katlian went to the Russian camp. He was accompanied by Nami and a small group of warriors. Lisianski accompanied him. To Katlian's amazement, the Russian leader, Lord Baranof, attended the peace talks. However, he did not address Katlian directly this day, but instead was consulted by Lisianski during the talks. This meeting was more decorous than significant. Their Russian leaders were dressed in their finest uniforms, complete with bicorn hats on their heads, and swords hanging at their sides. Lisianski cut an impressive and dashing figure as he stood with Katlian, who was not dressed for battle but instead wore his finest clothing, as did Nami.

The meeting took place at the former Tlingit camp at Castle Hill. This camp was abandoned by the Tlingit soon after the Russians returned, as they consolidated their forces in their new fort.

"We tire of war and seek peace," Katlian said. He said it in Russian, which raised some eyebrows among the Russian soldiers in attendance. That one sentence held the most important words spoken that day. Terms were exchanged that included the Tlingit's agreement to abandon and withdraw from their new fort the following day.

Unknown to the Russians, the Tlingit had already begun their withdrawal. Women and children had been leaving secretly at night, moving to their camp at old Sitka, several miles to the north.

■ ■ ■

Snow paid the lunch bill and he and his mother slowly walked off the meal en route to Lanny's house. Both enjoyed a smoke during their stroll. It was a pleasant afternoon and was not raining. They passed the historic Russian Bishop's house, painted yellow, as they strolled down Lincoln Street. They went into the small shrine-like room where they had talked before and sat to chat one last time. Just as Lanny was about to begin the conclusion of her story, she looked in the direction of the darkened doorway.

"Kee! Happy to see you," Snow said and got up. He was happy to see her for some reason. He had grown fond of her, but it was hard to know why.

Snow wanted to get a better look at her on this last day in Sitka. He went and stood in front of her, a couple feet away. He gave Kee a little bow and said, "I am glad to see you before I go."

Snow could see her a bit better than he had before, now that he was closer. He thought that she was an attractive woman in her late twenties or early thirties. But her lack of hygiene obscured her fine features.

"We will talk again when you return. I have seen it!" Kee said and gave a short rattle.

"Good to know. Thanks for the warning," Snow joked and then he impulsively gave her a hug.

Kee did not return the gesture, standing stiffly. Snow noticed when he hugged her that she felt quite thin. Before, her aroma was not quite what one would call off-putting, but it was a distinctive and unusual smell, something Snow did not want to linger on. He quickly wheeled away and returned to his seat.

"So Katlian met to talk about terms for peace, when in fact they had already begun their retreat?" Snow asked Lanny.

"That's right," Lanny said.

"That Katlian was something. He must have had incredible nerves to engage in talks with the enemy while his people had already begun their retreat. It seems that Katlian was one step ahead of Baranof and the Russians during the course of the Battle of Sitka. Every step of the way."

"It seemed to be true. The Russian historical accounts are different in the telling, but the basic facts don't seem to be in dispute. Just how they are presented, I guess," Lanny said.

That night, the Tlingit held their last gathering in the Shís'gi Noow—the Sapling Fort, as some called it. Many of the old, young, and women had already departed. The gathering included a long and loud drum roll and songs mourning the dead. But also, songs of praise at the successful defeat of the Russians and defense of their home. The Russians would interpret the sounds from the camp as a sign of the Tlingit surrender. The rest of the Tlingit left that night and melted into the woods.

The Russians came ashore the next morning and were surprised to discover that the Tlingit were gone. "That is the end of the Battle of Sitka," Lanny said. Kee shook her rattle. "The next chapter of this story is the Survival March of the Kiksadi. But we can save that for another day if you want to hear more," Lanny concluded.

They observed a couple moments of silence to mark the end of the story.

"Thank you for telling me the story, Lanny," Snow said. "But why did you tell me the story about Katlian? I mean, you could have told me anything, about your history and life. Your family. Instead, you decided to tell me about Katlian. Why is that?"

"I don't know," Lanny said after a thinking a bit. She sat silent, looking sad, gathering her thoughts. Snow pressed on.

"Why didn't you tell me more about your life, Mother? Did you think I would judge you?" Snow said.

Lanny again took some time before answering.

"Maybe a little bit," she said. "But that's not it. My life has been full of ups and downs. And the down periods were bad. With age, I have learned that the mistakes and hardships are part of me. They made me a better person. I am humbler. I am more empathetic and compassionate, I think, because of the dark times," Lanny said. "But the real reason was that I did not want to think about some of the things that happened, simply because it makes me so sad. Giving up my baby boy, you, that was something that haunted me for years. It was a stain on my soul. I did not want to open that wound, and others."

"I'm sorry, Mother. I did not intend to open any wounds. I was simply curious why you told me the story of Katlian," Snow said.

"I wanted you to know something about your heritage which I don't think you have learned yet," Lanny said. "And that is we have suffered great loss. You may think about that in an abstract way, but for us, it's not abstract. We have had things taken from us for generations. That loss is also part of your heritage."

"So, in part, the story of Katlian is a story of our loss, but also of our determination to fight. The pride we have in our heritage," she said.

"I understand," Snow said. "But I am struggling with something, though, on a personal level. I did not know my own race or history. For all of my life, I have not known. While it may seem curious to you, I became comfortable with that. I came to view it as an advantage," Snow said.

"Really? How so?" Lanny asked.

"I felt like people could not put me into some box, and even I could not put myself into a box. That helped me to feel neutral, like I had no agenda, and it's something that I became accustomed to and saw as an advantage. I was unaffiliated, like Switzerland, you know. Neutral," Snow rambled.

"I developed an idea that the exaggerated pride people take in their culture is part of the problem we face. Like that pride adds to the racial disfunction we are facing," Snow said.

"You are wrong. Well, mostly wrong. Pride in one's culture is fine; it's a good thing. Only if it is used as a bludgeon to assert oneself as better than others does it become a problem. Part of the pride we have in our culture is part of our way of saying, *We are not less than others*. Does that make sense?"

Kee rattled loudly.

Snow shook his head, like he was grappling with her statements.

"You were raised White. So, you are not familiar with the sense of loss in our culture, and of other cultures. So, you look at Native pride or BLM, for example, as part of the problem, perhaps. But you don't see the Saint Patty's Day celebrations as a problem, am I right?" Lanny asked.

Snow tilted his head to one side, thinking about what Lanny was saying.

After a minute of silence, Lanny said, "Why did you start the Tribal Court in Togiak?"

"My job. The mayor asked me to," Snow responded.

"Sure!" Lanny said with a laugh.

"I was told that you simply would not give up on it. There were a number of obstacles. And that you have continued to not only support the court but are helping drive it," Lanny said. "You were aware of systemic racism? Or at least aware that Natives have been disproportionately affected, right?"

"A person would have to be blind to not see that Natives and other minorities are ground up by the system. Treated unfairly. It's not just racism, though there is that. Nor is it simply a police thing, though that is an issue as well. But its poverty, substance and alcohol abuse, lack of access to education and jobs, just a broad array of issues," Snow said. "But you give me more credit than I deserve. I have an awareness, but I was not trying to address those broader problems. They are simply too big, too complex."

"I think differently," Lanny said. "I think you were aware of those things and were trying to address them."

"I was just trying to be a good police chief. Help the village address their problems. And they really wanted a Tribal Court, which I thought was critical. I mean, it would likely be successful, I thought, because the people really wanted it," Snow said.

"But the court did address some of the things you mentioned, right?" Lanny asked.

"Well, yes, it did, but it seemed to happen organically. The kids heard things in their own tongue and from their Elders. They heard of life in the old days, how hard it was. And how the people were able to pull together when challenged," Snow said.

"And?" Lanny asked.

"I think the kids heard more about their own culture. A sense of respect for their Elders and the ways of their culture," Snow added.

"And?" Lanny asked again.

"And what?" Snow asked, in frustration.

"Pride," Lanny said.

Snow got a look of suddenly getting what she was driving at.

"Oh, wow. Gee, I hate it when I defeat my own argument!" Snow said with exasperation.

Lanny and Snow both laughed at that.

"I respect your feelings, son. And I appreciate your willingness to have an open mind when it can be challenging to do so," Lanny said. "This information you learned about your heritage, it does not have to be a burden to you or define who you are. You can still be Switzerland."

CHAPTER 14
THE RETURN

Chief Snow met with Detective Alex Ramos and Senator Tom Begich in Anchorage on his return trip to Togiak.

"How was the trip to Sitka, Chief? You get to see your mother?" Tom Begich asked.

"It was great, Tom, thanks for asking. I appreciate your help getting me to Sitka. I met my birth mother there and we spent a few days together. I learned a lot of my Native heritage and Sitka's past."

"Good to hear, Chief. Job well done in finding Mary Frank. After we arrested Jon Brown and Mary Frank was medically cleared to go home, everyone returned to Togiak."

"I can arrange another trip down to Sitka for you, Chief. I have some work for you at the Police Academy if you are up for it," Begich offered.

"Well, I don't know, Tom. I appreciate the offer, but I don't know what my boss out in Togiak would say about that."

"I already talked to Mayor Moses and let him know about the successful operation in Anchorage. I asked him if he could spare you for a few more days to do some work for me, and he agreed, wholeheartedly," Begich said.

"You know Mayor Moses?" Snow asked. He knew that Begich had traveled to Togiak but was surprised he knew Mayor Moses well enough to give him a call. And was also surprised that Begich would advocate for him in this way.

"Sure, I've known Moses for years. I am trying to convince him to run for a state legislative seat. He would be good," Begich said.

"Is there anyone you don't know in this state?" Snow joked. It seemed that Begich had an encyclopedic network of contacts around the state. And not just politicians.

Begich smiled. "I been barnstorming around the state since I was a kid with my dad," he responded. "And Anchorage is my home twenty, so naturally I know a lot of people there too."

"I grew up there too, but you seem to know ten times more people than I do," Snow said.

"Well, my job is politics these days, and that often means meeting and remembering people," Begich explained.

"Your mother is Lanny Brady? I know her. Her family has quite a history in Tribal politics in Southeast," Begich said.

"You know Lanny? Why am I not surprised? As it turned out, she is related to this Chief Katlian guy who fought with the Russians back in the day," Snow said.

"I didn't know that but am not surprised by it. She had been a strong voice for women's rights, and for Native rights in this state," Begich said.

Chief Snow felt a rush of pride.

"Wow, you are related to Lanny and even Chief Katlian? That's pretty cool. He is a legend in the state, I am surprised you had not heard about him before," Begich said.

"Well, I probably did, but it did not stick. I won't forget now. The story Lanny told me was remarkable," Snow said.

"How about your time at the academy? Do anything exciting?" Alex asked. "I usually go down there a couple times a year to talk to the recruits about drug investigations. The recruits also like stories about the crazy policing stuff that happens in the bush," the detective said. "They love bear stories."

"I've got plenty of those," Snow said. "Not long ago, a bear came close to the village and chased a guy up a tree."

"I heard about that one!" Alex said. "Wasn't it the town vet?"

"I think I know that guy," Begich said.

"Right. That was it," Snow said. "The vet took his dogs walking and one of them lagged behind. He went to look for it and saw a blood trail. He followed the blood trail and came face to face with a bear. He was able to get up a tree and called for help on his cell phone," Snow said. "This vet is quite the character, I will say. I mean, he did not seem to be rattled by being chased by a bear at all. He was just worried about his missing dog," Snow said.

"Was this on the Cross Trail?" Begich asked.

"Exactly. The Cross Trail, near the trail headed down Indian River," Snow said, surprised that Begich knew the detail about where the bear was at.

"So, what happened to the dog?" Alex asked.

"The dog was killed by the bear who had already kind of covered it up to cache it for later. That's what they do."

"We found the dog, alright," Snow continued. "A group of us then followed the bear sign. The fish cops were there and had already decided that the bear would have to be put down. It was in town, attacked a dog, and chased a person, end of story.

"It's an unfortunate thing, but they put safety to people first. So, we tracked the bear until we were able to locate it and the wildlife trooper shot it with a bear gun that sounded like a frigging cannon. After the first shot, I think all of us shot a round or two; it was kind of like a shooting gallery for a few seconds. The bear was a pretty large one, they said."

"Wow. I thought chasing bad guys was kinda hairy. Can't imagine facing down a bear," Begich said. Snow thought about the close encounter he had after the plane crash, when he was mauled by a bear, but he didn't mention it.

"Chief Snow was attacked and mauled by a bear before when he was in a plane crash," Begich said. Snow was not even sure Begich knew about his incident with the bear. He was getting over being surprised by the depth of Begich's information. He wondered, what's next. *Is he going to start talking about Kinka too?*

"Holy shit, Snow!" Alex said and asked for the details. He told her the well-worn tale of the bear attack, except for the part about Kinka, and finished by showing her the claw marks on his chest and bicep.

"Can I touch it?" Alex asked.

"Sure, just don't tell Lilly!" Snow joked.

Alex traced the lines of the white claw scars on his bicep, but not the ones on his chest. Her touch was cool, and her fingers felt dainty on his skin. He was instantly aroused by her touch and had to squish that feeling immediately. He quickly changed the subject.

"We also had to fly on a helo over to Baranof Warm Springs to pick a guy up who had been stabbed," Snow said as he put his shirt back on.

"Yeah, I heard about that. In fact, I was the one who suggested that you go on the mission," Begich said. "I thought your background in fishing and work in the village might be helpful."

"Gee, thanks," Snow scoffed. "They lowered me down from the Coast Guard chopper in a basket in total darkness to a small dock where the victim was at. My butt cheeks are still a little puckered up over that."

"I guess they were worried the perp might still be hanging around. That was why I went down first, just in case he tried something. But he was hiding out in the woods, we discovered later," Snow said.

"The thing is, what they don't tell you is the basket spins as its going down. It's kind of disorienting," Snow said. "I don't think anyone ever volunteers doing it a second time, unless you are nuts or in the Coast Guard, which is kind of the same thing," Snow said with a smile. He had an immense respect for the Coast Guard; everyone in Alaska did. They were the crazy heroes who plucked people off sinking boats and the sides of mountains. He couldn't resist to dig them a little, though; it was kind of a universal cop thing to bust the balls of other agencies.

"After me, they lowered down a medic, who did the real work. I was just protection, I suppose," Snow continued. "The victim survived but it was kind of touch and go. It could have been fatal; he was stabbed multiple times, one time very close to the heart."

"Did you get the bad guy?" Alex asked.

"Yeah, but not right away. A trooper boat came over at first light with a few people from the AST and the Sitka Police Department. We searched around for a bit, but it was pretty clear he was hiding in the woods, and we were not going to be able to track him. I figured he was watching us and would come out if we left. I mean, he was probably getting pretty cold being in the woods all night. So, we kind of made a big show of leaving, but a couple of us stayed behind. We were hiding in the only store out there, and waited after the boat took off," Snow said.

"Hey, I know the guy who runs that store!" Begich said, to no one's surprise. "Whose idea was it to take off and leave a couple folks behind?" Begich asked.

"Well, it was kind of a group decision," Snow said.

"Not what I heard. Troopers are giving you credit for that," Begich said.

"Gee, that's nice of them. Anyways, we did not have to wait long. He came out of the woods almost immediately after the boat left. He was wet and cold, and we arrested him without a fight. Think he was pooped, and a little surprised we were there. Anyways, he came in easy. Charges for attempted murder, sounds like. It was a conflict on a boat they worked on together, which is actually pretty common," Snow concluded. He could tell lots of stories about things that happened on boats in Alaska.

"Where are we in the Jon Brown investigation?" Snow asked, tired of talking about his stuff, anxious to change the subject.

"Making progress," Alex said.

"Mary gave an excellent affidavit. I was hoping to get Jon Brown to talk so we could roll up his entire operation, but he's too streetwise to say anything, just lawyered up. The surprise came when Red decided to talk," Alex explained.

"Really? I didn't think he would roll on his buddies," Begich said.

"Turns out, he really does not want to go to jail. So, he is basically working for us at this point. He is kinda soft after all," Alex said.

"He flipped on Jon Brown?" Snow said.

"Yes sir. Jon Brown is toast, I do believe. And we got some names of people in villages they worked with to get girls," Alex said. "Seems as though Red was the primary recruiter, not Jon Brown."

Alex looked at Snow. "The name James Pook mean anything to you?"

"Oh, yeah. He's a piece of work, for sure, and plenty capable of what you are talking about. He's a bad actor, but he is limping a bit these days, I would imagine," Snow said with a smile. "Lilly shot him in the leg not long before we came to town!"

"Shut the front door. Really?" Begich said.

"Yeah, he was drunk and shot up the outside of the Round House where Lilly and I stay in Togiak. Much to his surprise, Lilly plugged him in the leg. Much to my surprise, too!" Snow said.

"Wow, I knew that chick was tough!" Alex said.

"He's in jail for a long stretch, I would imagine, so you shouldn't have any problem finding him," Snow said.

"He's not in jail," said Alex. "At least, I don't think so. Red was able to get through to him on his cell phone. Text, actually. He was able to corroborate that Pook had a hand in selecting Mary Frank and sending her into Anchorage," Alex said.

"I doubt he is out of jail. I mean, he was facing a number of serious charges. Shit, I hope they didn't let him out. I am worried about what he might do if he is loose in the village," Snow said.

The information about Pook had come about after Stanley Beans and Lilly had left town with Mary Frank, heading back to Togiak.

"Shit. I mean, that is good for the investigation. I am just worried about Lilly," Snow said. "I need to let Lilly and Stanley know to be careful if Pook is out. I better get back to Togiak ASAP."

■ ■ ■

Snow went for a walk to make a couple calls to Togiak. Lilly did not pick up, so he shot her a text. He called the police station and talked to Stanley. He told him to be careful and watch out for James Pook. Stanley said that he was aware Pook was back but apparently Pook was laying low. At least there had been no complaints or reports of him raising hell.

"Just be careful. And keep an eye out for Lilly, too, can you? That guy worries me, especially if he is looking at doing some real time," Snow said.

He got on the Alaska Airlines website and set up his flight back for the next morning. The one flight heading to Dillingham was already gone, so he would need to wait.

Snow came back from his walk and smoke. Begich and Alex were chatting and suddenly stopped when he walked up.

Snow smiled, figuring they must have been talking about him. "What?" he said to them both.

"I was telling Alex I thought you would be a good addition to her state task force on sex trafficking," Begich said.

"Don't know about that. I mean, I got into two fights in like two days. Besides, Detective Ramos can be kinda mean," Snow said to Begich, grinning.

"She actually is the one who brought it up," Begich said. Alex nodded in agreement.

"Yes, I did. We could use someone who knows how things work, or don't work, out in the villages," Alex said.

"And I need someone to help with the new Crime Lab," Begich said, referring to the Alaska State Scientific Crime Detection Laboratory located in Anchorage. Most people referred to is simply as the Crime Lab.

The Crime Lab processed evidence or provided analysis from the entire state and did everything from DNA analysis to identifying controlled substances, or fingerprints to footwear impressions in the snow or elsewhere.

"Crime Lab? I don't know anything about the Crime Lab," Snow said to Begich.

"Sure you do. You know how to do sexual assault kits, collect DNA and fingerprints, and properly submit things to the lab," Begich said.

"We need to train village officers on those things. And with major investigations, at times. I mean, they get it in the academy, but it's such a blizzard of information when they are going through, by the time they get out there and are working, they forget they have resources, the Crime Lab, to help with criminal cases. So, you could help educate the village officers. It would be a good excuse for you to travel out to villages, which would also help you work some cases with Alex or support on other major investigations. And you could come down to Sitka on occasion, to the academy," Begich explained, but he was hinting that Snow would be able to see his mother.

"I already have a job," Snow said. "And, well, I mean, Lilly would have to be on board."

"Yeah, I suppose she would be heartbroken leaving Togiak," Begich said sarcastically.

"Well, she would probably be okay leaving the village. But she has a job. And where would I be based? And I feel like I still have a lot of things to do in Togiak. A lot of questions, but I am very flattered," Snow said. "I would need extra pay if I am working for Alex. She's a beast. Like hazard pay or something."

Alex did not blink at the sass from Snow; it was just one cop digging another. Standard operating procedure.

"Well, he's a handful, headstrong, and opinionated," Alex started digging back at Snow, but then stopped, turning serious. "It would be a great chance to do some good in the state, Snow. I don't have to tell you what the numbers are up here. I know we could make a great team. I feel pretty good about that. I think you could really help our effort," she said. "Besides, ain't you getting tired of chasing bears around?" she asked with a smile.

Alex, Begich, and Snow sat for a while, talking about the possibilities and what this could look like, and how it might work. He liked the idea of working on something new and different.

"You may be able to work with Tribal Courts too. You may get some Tribal Courts to take a shot at working with some of the sexual abuse cases. I mean, it may seem like a stretch, but they've had some success doing just that in some remote Inuit villages in Canada," Begich said.

"I thought about that too," Snow said. "If you really want to stop the sexual abuse, you need to get the villagers involved, the Elders. You need the community to say what is unacceptable behavior. I could see situations where the Elders may take a shot at rehabilitation to keep offenders in the village instead of losing them to the correctional system."

"That's it exactly. I know many law enforcement types would not be too thrilled about that. Most just want to lock them up and throw away the key. But I figured you might see it differently," Begich said. That gave Snow some pause. It meant something, but he was not sure if it was a good thing or not.

"I mean, I am flattered. And it does sound pretty good. The job description just expanded to be pretty daunting, but that does not scare me too much," said Snow.

"Let's talk in a couple weeks. You talk to Lilly. By the way, I imagine we could probably find something for Lilly too. I mean, she is an experienced nurse; I think most villages could use help or some training. She may be able to travel with you on legit work for the various village clinics. Let me check that out with some of our DHS folks," Begich said, referring to the Department of Health and Social Services.

"Holy crap, Tom, you've thought of everything!" Snow said.

"Well, I happen to think this would be a good fit. I am not just thinking of you, by the way. I am thinking about the problems we face in this state with sexual assault and the rest of it, and how best to combat them. I want to use you," Begich joked.

"Use and abuse. I'm used to it, man!" Snow responded.

It was agreed they would touch base in a couple weeks.

Later that night, Chief Snow was able to get in touch with Lilly on the phone. They talked about the job prospect and what it would mean. The conversation shifted to the language of love.

"So, will you marry me?" Snow asked Lilly.

"You are going to ask me to marry you on the phone?" she said.

"Well, I am on my knees," Snow said, bending on one knee.

"Gee, I don't know. I never expected to be proposed to over the phone. I guess it's better than a text," Lilly said, giggling. It gave Snow hope that she didn't simply say no and was laughing.

"You are right. I shouldn't ask you on the phone," Snow said and promised to ask her in person. He was already thinking about how best to do that.

"Be careful about Pook," was the last thing he said to her.

CHAPTER 15
KIDNAPPED

Lilly was happy to be back at work, and the clinic was busy. It seemed as though some folks were waiting for her to come back to the clinic for whatever ailment they had. Lilly had quietly assumed a leadership role in the small clinic. They used to have a physician assistant, or PA, but the PA had unfortunately flamed out pretty quick and left in a hurry.

The loss of the PA had been mitigated by the increasing use and availability of video conferencing and other methods of getting professional input in the village on medical issues. Because Lilly had already worked in Dillingham, she had relationships with the doctors on staff at Kanakanak hospital. This factor enhanced her status at the clinic in Togiak.

Lilly decided to take a late lunch and walk to the Round House. She expected her boyfriend to be back in an hour or two. She knew he made it to Dillingham and was waiting to catch a flight over to Togiak. She had freed up her schedule for a couple hours so she could eat lunch and hopefully meet Snow when he got back to the village.

Lilly announced her intentions to her coworkers and put on her jacket. It was beginning to warm up in Togiak, so she had switched from the parky she normally wore to a lighter puffy jacket. Lilly checked her face in the mirror of the clinic bathroom before heading out the door. She saw the swelling was gone and her face looked pretty normal. She had some light bruising on her left cheek, but it had simply turned a light shade of yellow and was hard to see. Satisfied with her face, she headed out.

Lilly stopped first at the AC Store and shopped around for a bit, eventually grabbing some hot pockets to take home for lunch. She missed the everything salad bar at the Carrs store in Anchorage. She could go for a nice salad, but that was not anything you could ever get in Togiak.

Lilly was lost in thought as she walked on the right side of the gravel road toward her destination, the Round House. She thought about how life had changed so much in the past year or so. She met her boyfriend, Brady Snow, the Togiak police chief, after he had been mauled by the bear. After he had been in a place crash.

She remembered the time they met with fondness. She and Brady would often talk about it. Brady would laugh and say the first words she said to him were, "Are you married?" When Brady said he was not married, she asked him, "Are you sure?" It was one of those moments that seem to freeze in time for both of them. It made her smile just thinking about it. She thought about how he had courted her in his own way. And the time he had come to Dillingham and met her family.

Lilly had strong feelings about Brady Snow from the get-go. There was something there, almost tangible between them. She could feel it. There was an attraction, a sexual tension to be sure, and it was a strong attraction. But there was something else she felt when they met too. She had the simple feeling that he was a good man, not going to deceive or hurt her. She knew better than to simply trust that feeling, but it was there, and she felt it. The combination of those feelings had been a bit disarming the night they met.

But when he came to Dillingham and spent time with her Oppa, her feelings about Brady changed. She had spied on them when they were chatting in the living room of the house she lived in with her Oppa. The way he treated her Oppa so respectfully was important to her. But it was the sudden warming to him, and the respect given by her Oppa back to Brady, that made the real impact. They talked to each other easily and as if they were equals. Her Oppa even showed Brady his bear scars on his butt. She was not quite prepared for that, because it was unprecedented for her to see any of that. Her Oppa was, by nature, reserved, so to see him so comfortable and at ease with Brady was something she had not witnessed with anyone, let alone any of her suitors who were brave enough to come to the house and walk the gauntlet. It changed her thoughts about Brady; suddenly her feelings took on more depth.

Lilly was smart, sharper than she let on. She knew about men. She knew that Brady was a good man, but he was still a man. Men wanted sex; it was simply a fact of life. And women did too, but some men were obsessed with it. They would charm for it, take it by force, wine and dine, just about anything to get it. It could be a challenge to filter out the sexual tension and male obsessiveness to get down to the nitty gritty of a man's real character.

The interaction between her Oppa and Brady saved her a lot of time trying to sift through the detritus and smokescreens men would throw up in their quest for sex. She knew at that moment that Brady was a good person, with good character. She knew it. Her Oppa did not need to say anything to her formally about Brady; she knew that he had not only vetted him, but liked and approved of him too. She had heard Snow tell her Oppa about meeting an Enukin, or Little People—Kinka the Kinda. And her Oppa had been impressed as they chatted about that. She remembered fondly when Snow somehow sensed her watching and looked over at her. She was going to turn away but did not. Instead, they both stared at each other for some moments before the spell was broken. Looking back at it, she felt that was the exact moment she fell in love.

That night, and how her Oppa and Brady seemed to not only get along but hold each other in high regard, changed things for Lilly. It made life much easier for her in her budding relationship with Brady. She no longer felt the need to be so guarded with Brady. And once that happened, she fell in love. Hard. It was a rapid transition from guarded attraction to a blossoming romance. And the passion! She was not prepared for that either. She had sex before, but she now understood that there was sex and then there was unbridled passion with someone you love. It was like the difference between a blade of grass and a bouquet of roses.

She and Brady had tentatively explored their sexual attraction together. Both were a bit shy in that regard. In some ways, she was more secure than he. She remembered with a smile the first time she had stayed over at the Round House. Brady was in taking a shower, and she simply disrobed and joined him in the shower. It was kind of impulsive on her part, but it also felt totally natural. She thought Brady was going to burst a blood vessel, he was so surprised! *That shower had a very happy ending,* she thought with a smile.

The past year had been filled with love and adventure. It had been the fullest year of her young life. Even the potentially bad things, like the close call in Anchorage, and Jon Brown's scary assault. Or James Pook shooting up the Round House. And her response of shooting him in the leg! For some reason, nothing seemed to faze her or frighten her during this time in her life. It was crazy, for sure, but she was in this cocoon of love that seemed to soften or obliterate any fears she would normally have. Now she was working as a valued nurse in the village. She knew they needed her, and it felt good to be able to help. It seemed like her life was a wild adventure, suddenly, and she and Brady were in the center of it all. It was crazy fun and exciting.

■ ■ ■

James Pook and his cousin JJ had already been drinking as Pook drove back into town after watching the caribou up in the hills again.

"We need to go hunting before they move, I suppose," JJ said. But he was already half lit so it was simply a statement. It was not going to happen today, and they both knew it.

"Eeee, we'll go soon," Pook responded.

Then something happened that changed the course of several lives. It was simply fate that Lilly, JJ, and Pook were all in the same place at the same time. Lilly could have skipped the store or gotten a ride. Pook and JJ could have stayed a bit longer one way or the other or taken a different route through the village. But they didn't.

Pook took a left near the police station, and there she was— Lilly walking down the right side of the road, alone. Pook looked around and did not see anyone behind him or coming in his direction. He did not see anyone outside. He also did not see the Elder Annie Blue standing in the doorway of her house smoking a cigarette. Pook was zeroed in on Lilly now. He did not hear the plane overhead, buzzing loudly to signify a landing.

He acted spontaneously, like he usually did. After he had thought about something at length, he usually had already made up his mind about it. If the opportunity presented itself, he would simply act on his impulse without hesitation.

Pook swerved in front of Lilly and jumped out of the truck. He yelled, "You drive!" to JJ.

Lilly was taken off guard by the sudden attack. If she had been more alert, she may have been able to run away. As it was happening, she was walking along kind of in a daze. When she saw Pook coming at her, she turned to run, but he was on her before she even made a couple steps. He simply picked her up and carried her the few feet to the truck.

Lilly began to scream and flail, to fight back. Pook slammed her into the side of the truck, then opened the door with his left hand as he held Lilly with his right. Pook picked her up to throw her into the back seat. Lilly managed to get her right leg against the side of the truck to brace herself. But Pook was heavy and strong and overwhelmed her. She tumbled into the back seat, with Pook landing on her.

"Go! Drive!" Pook hollered at JJ who had clambered into the driver's seat.

"Where we going?"

"Hunting cabin!" Pook hollered.

Lilly was struggling and looking for some way to get out from underneath Pook. She could hardly move. She was screaming, "Help! Help me!"

Pook roughly brought his right arm through, and then over her face to muffle her screams, but he did it so roughly it was like a blow across her face. She was jammed down into the back seat of the truck along with hunting clothes, a shotgun, trash, and other miscellaneous items. She spied the shotgun on the floorboard. She wondered if she could get to it, a Remington 870 pump action, the same gun Pook had used to shoot up the Round House. She saw a half empty box of bright red shells on the floor.

JJ drove past the Round House and onto the beach. He was heading north to a hunting cabin he often used.

"Stop! Stop it! I can't breathe!" Lilly screamed into the seat. She was face down in the back seat with Pook on top of her. She was tiring and very frightened.

"Shut up!" Pook said angrily and cuffed the back of her head a couple times with his right hand. Lilly moved her head back and forth to try and avoid being hit, moaning in pain.

"You asked for this, bitch! I told you!" Pook said.

Pook felt exhilaration. And sexually aroused. He did not get aroused by his wife anymore, unless he took her forcefully. Raped her. His sexual desires had become intertwined with violent dominance.

He had done it. He had gotten Lilly and was going to make her pay for shooting his leg, and get back at that frigging snowflake cop.

Lilly was in shock and was tired and hurting. She had stopped struggling. *Think!*

■ ■ ■

Old Tribal Judge Annie Blue had been standing in her doorway; she was going to have a smoke. She knew she shouldn't smoke, but still liked to have one on occasion. She was sneaky about it, because she was a bit ashamed of the old habit that lingered. She would sneak a smoke when the grandkids were in school, or she was home alone for one reason or another. Mostly, she did not want to be a bad example for the young people. But a smoke, occasionally, sure tasted good.

Annie was in her eighties. But her hair was still black, and she still had her own teeth. Her mind was sharp, mental acuity not lost. She was one of those remarkable people with the right genes that kept them healthy and vibrant well past other folks of similar age. She attributed it to her diet, which was almost completely traditional Native foods, like dried fish and seal oil, which she loved.

Annie took a drag on her smoke, followed the exhaled smoke's trail with her eyes just as Pook's truck swerved in front of Lilly. Even though she didn't really see Lilly's face that well, she knew it was Lilly. Same thing with Pook.

If you live in a small town and see the same folks day after day, you get to know their clothing, their vehicles, their mannerisms, and other things that identify them. You can tell who someone is just by how they walk, or their clothes, or by some other personal characteristic. She recognized Pook's clothing and his truck. She also saw JJ driving.

Annie saw Pook violently pick her up and slam her against the truck. Her eyes got big as she watched Pook load her into the truck. She could hear Lilly's screams. Annie Blue watched the truck pull away.

She picked up her mobile phone from the little shelf inside the door. She kept her phone on the shelf when she smoked so she did not miss a call. The same shelf was also where she kept an ashtray, cigarettes, and a lighter. She called the police.

■ ■ ■

Chief Snow was dozing as he rode in the plane. He was with his favorite bush pilot, Chubby Libbits. He and Chubby chatted a bit while they loaded some freight, and then Chubby did his checks before takeoff.

Chubby said, "Let's go, we're burning daylight!" Snow smiled at the phrase. Chubby always said that, and now Snow did too. They were airborne in a flash. Chubby was chewing on a cigar stump as he talked to Snow. It was not a pretty sight, that cigar; it was better not to look too close at the soggy stogie.

"I heard you found that little girl in Anchorage. You and Lilly. Everyone is talking about it. That's a good thing!" Chubby said.

"Eeee, that's right. Stanley Beans helped a lot too. He knows his way around Anchorage pretty good," Snow said as they flew south and west away from Dillingham toward Togiak.

"She okay now?" Chubby asked.

"I think she will be. She was kind of on her own for a while, got mixed up in some stuff in the big town. I hope she stays home now, goes back to school," Snow said.

"Never can tell. We lose a lot of the kids who go to town to work or . . . you know," Chubby said.

That was true. Often kids went to Anchorage or Fairbanks for college or just looking for work. Some came back to stay, but many did not. And, of course, they lost people, not just kids, to the life in the fast lane of the big towns. *It had been refreshing to go out to restaurants and go the mall*, Snow mused. He wondered to himself about moving there. Taking the job Begich had talked about. He had a lot to talk to Lilly about.

■ ■ ■

Stanley Beans was getting ready to go to the airport to meet his boss. He was listening to the radio and heard Chubby announce his approach. He knew the flight was close when he got a text from Chief Snow asking for a ride into town, then he heard the plane overhead buzzing the town. Chubby practically rattled the windows in the police station.

"That'll wake up Mr. Beans!" Chubby barked in the plane, with a laugh that sounded like a cat choking up a hairball. Snow smiled. This was exactly why he liked Chubby. He had a simple joy for life, though at times it might come at someone else's expense.

■ ■ ■

Inside the police station, the phone rang just as Stanley had his hand on the doorknob. *Now what? Probably nothing, but you never know,* he thought. He was happy the Chief was back, so he did not have to worry so much.

"Lilly. She been kidnapped! I saw it!" Annie Blue said in a rush. Stanley recognized her voice.

"What? What happened, Annie?" Stanley asked.

"James Pook. Grabbed her and threw her in the truck. Looks bad, Stanley. He was rough with her. She was screaming!" Annie said. She was near tears at the violence she described.

"Eeee! Oh, sweet Jesus! Which way he go?" Stanley asked.

"Looked like he went up the beach, upriver to the hunting cabins, probably. JJ was in the truck too! He's driving! Think they're cooked," she added, meaning she thought they were drunk. "You need to do something, Stanley. They're going to rape her!" Annie said, now crying. Like most women in the bush, she had her own experience in such matters. She did not want anyone to go through that!

"Okay, Annie. Going to get Chief right now!" Stanley said and hung up. He jumped in the white police pickup and tore out of there in a rush, spinning the tires and throwing rocks as he sped away.

Stanley Bean could have gone off on his own to try and chase down Pook and find Lilly. But the airport was only a couple minutes away, so he decided it was better to go get the Chief. He would know what to do.

■ ■ ■

JJ was driving on the beach heading toward the hunting cabin. Things got a bit quiet in the truck for a few minutes.

"You don't have to do this. You can still let me go," Lilly said finally.

"Shut up! I told you I was going to teach you some manners! Now it's time for some payback. You shot me in the leg, in case you've forgotten!" Pook said into Lilly's hair. He was still on top of her, though both he and Lilly had shifted around some. Pook took his right hand and pushed Lilly's head down hard onto the seat.

"Almost there," JJ said, looking in the rearview mirror. "I need a drink!"

The real reason for him being along was to get some booze. He actually liked Lilly and secretly hoped she would not get hurt.

"Me too!" Lilly said. This made both Pook and JJ laugh.

■ ■ ■

Snow was in kind of a trance as he watched the scenery out the window. The plane landed and pulled up abruptly to a stop. Stanley was standing by the battered old white ford pickup truck. He was waving his arms, looking like a jumping bean.

"Your boy looks kinda worked up!" Chubby commented. "Musta caught a shoplifter," Chubby joked. But Snow wasn't laughing. He was worried about why Stanley Beans was so worked up.

Chubby made his way to the back hatch and opened it up, swinging the collapsible steps down so they could exit. Stanley was standing right outside by the time the steps came down.

"Chief!!" he shouted. Snow poked his head out before descending the couple steps down to the gravel strip.

"They got Lilly!"

■ ■ ■

JJ drove up off the beach and over the bank on a trail that had been cut. It was pretty steep, but he had made this maneuver many times. Despite his alcohol impairment, he easily made it up the bank and parked next to the cabin. They always parked the truck in this spot; there was a place worn down in the long grass that was prevalent on the flats above the river.

Lilly was scheming, thinking of when to try and make a break for it, or how she could run away and hide in the long grass until help came. The trick was to pick the right moment. She would likely only get one shot at it, and after that, Pook would be wary. Or he would hurt her so she couldn't run.

Pook was thinking about taking Lilly sexually, raping her. That was a given, really. But right now, he was more interested in getting into the cabin so he could drink. He had a couple bottles of R and R with him.

"Get up!" Pook had opened the door behind him and grabbed Lilly hard by the arm and jerk her toward him.

He had her by both arms, his large hands grabbing her tight by the biceps through her coat.

"Ow, you're hurting me!" Lilly cried.

"Shut up!" he said and pushed her hard into the side of the truck, pulling her body aggressively toward him, his arms wrapped around her waist securely.

"You ain't going anywhere," he said as if reading her mind.

Pook half dragged, half carried, her into the cabin. He tossed her down into the homemade wooden bunk. He backhanded her across the face.

"That's just a warning. If you try anything stupid, I will wreck your face! You get it?!" Pook hollered.

Lilly nodded, her face hidden. She did not want Pook to see her tears.

Pook went to the truck and grabbed his shotgun and shells and came right back in the cabin. Lilly thought she may have had a chance to run, but the moment had passed and Pook was back in the cabin.

Lilly looked around the cabin for anything she might be able to use as a weapon.

■ ■ ■

Chief Snow was deadly serious; he snapped into that mode when things got shitty. Although he did not enjoy being in action mode, he knew all about it and was very comfortable being in it. He knew it was one of his strongest assets as a police officer. Snow had the unusual ability to get calmer and more decisive when things got hairy. The worse the shit, the calmer he got. As long as he didn't let his emotions get in the way, he would be fine. That was going to be a challenge this time, he knew. He was going to choke down and smother with a pillow any angry feelings or worries about Lilly; he wouldn't let it interfere with the job of rescuing her.

Chief Snow was worried and anxious. Part of him wanted to just jump in the truck and immediately start searching for Lilly. But he knew better. It was important at this moment to get as much information as he could, so he did not waste time later. He felt like this could be life and death, so needed to be under control to avoid mistakes. That meant taking a bit of crucial time to gather facts.

"Tell me, Stanley. Take your time and tell me what is going on," Snow said in a voice like he was talking about the weather.

"Eeee . . . Annie called. Pook took Lilly! In the truck. JJ too," Stanley stammered. He took a big gulp of air after each jumbled sentence. He was practically hyperventilating.

Snow put his arm on Stanley's shoulder.

"It's okay, everything will be fine, Stanley. I just need you to slow down, start at the beginning, and tell me what happened."

Chubby pulled in closer to hear Stanley. He knew Snow and Lilly both. In fact, Chubby Libbits knew just about everyone in these parts.

"Eeee," Stanley said and took a shaky inhale.

"Annie Blue called just when I was leaving to come and pick you up. I was going to not answer it, but I decided to anyways, thought *you never know* and answered the phone," Stanley began. Chubby and Snow exchanged a look.

"Okay, then what. What did Annie say?"

"Annie said she saw Pook's truck stop in front of Lilly. Pook jumped out and grabbed Lilly. Annie said he was rough with her and threw her down, or maybe she said he threw her against the truck. Yeah, that's it, he threw her against the truck."

"Then what?" Snow urged. "You are doing good."

"Um, Annie said Lilly was screaming and kicking too. But Pook picked her up and threw her in the back seat of the truck. He climbed in the back and was like holding her down."

"Go on, what happened next," Snow said.

"Annie said she saw JJ get into the driver's seat and drive away. Lilly and Pook were down in the back seat, and she could only see like the top of Pook's head," Stanley said.

"Good. Then what?" Snow asked.

"She saw them head toward the beach. She thinks they're heading to the cabin. Pook's hunting cabin. Upriver," Stanley said.

"Do we know for sure where they are at right NOW?" Chief Snow asked.

"Not for sure, no. Likely Pook's hunting cabin though, Annie thought so anyways. They were headed to the beach though," Stanley said.

Snow asked a couple more questions. But he was soon satisfied that was all Stanley knew.

"Eeee. This is all my fault. I never should have left her alone. I could've done something. I mean, I should've done something!" Stanley was almost sobbing.

"You did good. Now I need you to do a couple things while I am going to go get Lilly."

"I can help. I want to help," Chubby said. The old military man inside Chubby was suddenly awake and ready to go. Snow had never seen Chubby like this before. But he recognized that look; he had seen it before on the faces of law enforcement or military people.

"Good. I can use the help," Snow said.

Snow and Chubby talked intensely for about one minute. Chubby made some motions with his hands. Then suddenly Chubby nodded his head up and down and Snow walked toward the truck.

"Let's go, Stanley. I am driving," Snow said, and they hopped into the truck. Chubby climbed into the plane and pulled up the steps behind him.

■ ■ ■

Pook checked his shotgun over and laid it on the small table in the middle of the room. Then he pulled a box of shells out of his pocket and set it on the table. He pulled out a plastic brown bottle of R and R whiskey out of the inside pocket of his tan coat.

"I need a drink before I do anything else," Pook said. It was a new bottle and he had to break the plastic seal. Then he unscrewed the bottle and took a nice long pull. He made a face and waited for a minute or so, the bottle still in his hand. Then he took another smaller drink and put the cap back on the bottle and tossed it to JJ.

JJ unscrewed it and also took a nice big pull. Lilly hid her face with her arm, peeking out at JJ, thinking of asking him for a drink. She thought the half-wit might be her ticket out of this mess. She didn't think JJ was necessarily a bad person. In fact, he could be quite nice and seemed gentle. He had been very appreciative when she helped one of his children. She thought he was probably just mixed up in this so he could have some booze. And she was right about that, but he was up to his neck in it now.

Lilly peeked around the one room cottage. It looked to be about twelve square feet, which was typical for a hunting camp. There was a small window facing south, toward town, on one wall. That was the only window, and it looked too high up and too small to do much but look out. She would have to get out through the only door to the cabin. The walls were unpainted plywood, the color a bit brighter than the dull gray clouds outside. The roof was flat, also made of plywood. There was a bench of sorts, or a shelf about waist high under the window. On the bench were random items, a coil of rope which could prove useful, but nothing else of importance. She saw a couple traps hanging from nails on the wall. She might be able to use one of the metal traps for a weapon. The shotgun was on the table. She might have to wait for them to get drunk, then she could make a run for it, or maybe get the gun.

■ ■ ■

Snow pulled in at the police station. He was moving with purpose, but smoothly like he did when was he was in the zone. He went in and opened the gun safe. He had put his gun belt in the large safe meant for long guns. He put it in there for safe keeping while he was out of town. He snapped the belt around his waist and put the gun over it. He wore black jeans, meaning business. As his mission continued, his mind had conversations with itself.

They most likely have shotguns in the cabin, probably a hunting rifle too. I would imagine they are going to rape Lilly. They probably figured to take turns raping her until they decided to kill her. That might take a day or two. Pook must not have known he was coming, or they would not have done this today. It was probably just a spur of the moment thing. Hopefully they are busy getting drunk and I have some time.

Snow slid the .40-caliber black Glock pistol out of the holster and did a press check. He checked the magazine—fully loaded— then slammed it back into the gun, with the lower part of the palm of his left hand. He checked his belt and saw that he had two other full magazines. He was satisfied with the belt. He reached into the safe and pulled out the best 12-gauge shotgun, the one he liked the best. He checked the action and quickly loaded it with buckshot and three additional slugs into the ammo saddle on the side of the gun.

"Stanley. I need you to call the troopers. Don't give up until you talk to somebody over there in Dillingham. You need to tell them what is going on. And tell them we need help right away. Okay? Don't take no for an answer. Tell them Chief Snow said to come right way. Like immediately, *right* NOW. You got it?" Snow said to Stanley.

"Eeee, I got it. Call and get help. Right away. Lilly is in trouble. Eeee, I got it," Stanley said.

"If you talk to Sergeant Dickron or Trooper Roop, tell them I went upriver to Pook's hunting cabin. Look for his white pickup truck. Tell Big Dick that I went after her. Went after them. Got it?" Snow asked.

"Eeee, got it. Maybe you should wait for them to get here?" Stanley said.

"Can't. I could, but I can't. Might be safer if I waited, but they are going to hurt her. Pook is going to hurt her. I am going *now* to stop him. I am going now, I have to," Snow said as if he was trying to convince Stanley.

"I will come too!" Stanley said. He seemed about to cry. Snow again put his hand on Stanley's shoulder to buck him up. *Hang in there a bit longer, Stanley. I need you to hang in there just a little while longer,* he thought.

"No. I need you to stay and get in touch with the troopers. It's very important, the most important thing. I need you do that, okay?" Snow asked.

"Eeee," Stanley said.

"After that, you can follow along after me upriver. You should probably wait for the troopers if they are coming, so you can lead them to the cabin. But only after you get in touch with the troopers," Snow said. And he headed for the door.

CHAPTER 16
THE CABIN

Snow jumped on the four-wheeler out front. Out of habit, he rocked it back and forth as a means of checking the fuel. *Plenty of gas.* He slid the shotgun into the scabbard until it hit home. It was designed to be a bit tight to hold the gun in place without straps; it simply held the gun by gravity and being a nice snug fit.

Snow did a quick 180, then sped away from the police station, heading north. He drove past the Round House and onto the beach. He looked up and around, as if looking to the sky for help. Then he hit the throttle with his right thumb and picked up speed. He stayed in close to the cut bank as he drove north. The tide was out, so there was plenty of beach, but he wanted to stay in close to the bank. This would make him less visible from the cabin, he hoped. And it would also serve to muffle the sound of the four-wheeler as he got closer to the cabin. He was only going about half throttle to minimize the noise of the engine.

Inside the cabin, Lilly heard a machine in the distance. It made her hopeful, but she could not count on the sound being help on the way. She wanted to distract Pook and JJ. She sat up and loosened her coat a bit by zipping it down about halfway.

Pook took notice and stood in front of her, with his crotch pushed forward. He was getting hard, and made an adjustment in front of Lilly so she could plainly see what he was doing.

"I told you before. I am going to show you what it's like to be with a real man. I think it is time for your first lesson, girl," Pook said.

JJ looked drunk, but he was also starting to look uncomfortable. Unlike Pook, taking a woman with violence did not arouse him, nor did it appeal to him. And watching another man force himself on a woman made him sick to think about.

"Can I have a little sip, to get me in the mood?" Lilly said. This was not expected and made Pook laugh. She was looking at JJ when Pook laughed and hoped he could read her mind. She was trying to buy some time, any time, and hopefully get Pook more interested in booze. If he thought she was willing to have sex, maybe that would help her in some way.

"Yeah, let's drink!" JJ said. *He's going to help me,* Lilly thought!

"Nah! I'm feeling like you need to have some big cock, and I think it's right now," he said. "I know what you are doing, Lilly. You are trying to be tricky, hoping maybe to buy some time. But no one is coming to help you!" he said.

Pook pushed her down on the plywood bunk. He wanted to see her body.

"I am pregnant, though!" Lilly said.

"Good!" Pook responded. He was about to get rough, and it turned him on immensely. The violence was his aphrodisiac.

■ ■ ■

Chubby took off from the airport in his piper Cherokee. There had been some mail on the plane, not amounting to much weight, but he dumped it on the runway just to be safe.

Chubby climbed a bit and then banked to the south. He wanted a little elevation to see better. It worked. He saw Snow on the four-wheeler already nearing the cabin.

"Hold on! Wait for me!" Chubby said and put the plane into a steep dive. He had a smile and a soggy cigar stub in the corner of his mouth. He pulled up when he got very low.

Snow suddenly heard the plane and glanced to his left. Chubby was so low, like the plane was practically at eye level as it sped past on his left.

Chubby said, "Wake up, boys! HERE'S JOHNNY!"

He goosed the throttle several times right above the cabin. He was so low it seemed like his wheels would almost scrape the roof of the cabin. Chubby banked up and out over the water. The plane was sideways, as he went out over the water. He was going to make a tight turnaround and make another pass! In his mind, he was back in the Air Force flying a mission over hostile territory. Chubby adjusted his captain's hat with the scrambled eggs on the bill and headed back around.

Inside the cabin, the noise built as Chubby made his approach. Pook got up from the bunk where he had been about to school Lilly on the finer points of violent sex. He and JJ exchanged a look. Then suddenly the sound was deafening inside the cabin as Chubby buzzed directly overhead. It sounded like a freight train and actually shook the cabin and rattled the window.

Pook and JJ both rushed to the one window and looked out.

Lilly knew instantly that this was her moment. She got up suddenly and made a break for it. She quickly dismissed going for the shotgun, which lay unattended on the table. Instead, she made for the door.

Pook saw her out of the corner of his eye. Instead of chasing her, he hollered, "Get HER!" at JJ, who grabbed for her but bumped the table, knocking the shotgun to the floor. He staggered after Lilly, but she made it to the door and was out.

Snow was still on the beach, quickly approaching the cabin, needing to make a decision as to what to do. But then the door of the cabin flew open, and Lilly burst out into the open. *Lilly!* His eyes got wide. He saw JJ hot on her heals. Snow instantly drove to intercept JJ, veering right up the bank toward him. He was hoping to run into him and knock him down.

When he hit the bank at an angle, the four-wheeler went sideways in the air. Everything suddenly went into slow motion. Snow saw the machine launch slowly into the air and begin to turn under him. The four-wheeler seemed to slide out from under him as it turned sideways in the air. He and the machine were airborne.

Snow saw Pook in the doorway of the cabin, a shotgun in his hands aiming right at him!

BANG!

Snow was flying through the air; he still had his left hand on the handlebar of the four-wheeler as it slid out from under him, slowly inverted toward him. He felt and heard the buckshot pellets wiz by.

The four-wheeler's front wheel hit JJ and he went down, stunned. The machine landed on its side, right on the edge of the bank.

Snow had pulled his sidearm out with his right hand, his left on the seat of the crashed four-wheeler facing him. He heard the boom of the gun and heard pellets hitting the underside of the machine. He heard JJ moan as he was hit by pellets. Snow was hit on the left arm, but the pain didn't register. He brought his hands together on the gun and fired into the upper center of James Pook's chest, unsure whether he wounded him or not. Pook seemed unfazed.

At that moment, the plane came out of nowhere and flew impossibly low, lower than the roof of the shack, passing by Pook in a blur.

The wing of the plane barely missed Pook who was still standing just out of the doorway of the cabin holding his chest. Pook made an animal sound, like AHHHGG! As Chubby banked the plane sideways, Pook was up with his gun, following the plane with it, like he was shooting skeet. He fired a shot, and then another at the plane as it banked away.

Chubby thought he may have got Pook as he made the pass. But no such luck. He banked away and down toward the beach. He heard something hitting the plane on the underside. Then again near the tail. He was going to try and set down on the beach. His plane had been shot up.

"Drop the gun!" Snow shouted at Pook.

"Drop the gun!" Snow shouted again.

Pook racked the shotgun and raised it to shoot. Two shots rang out at the same time. Snow did not duck when Pook fired, and instead squeezed off another volley, which found its mark—right in the chest, dead center. Pook just stood there and looked down at his chest. He started to raise the shotgun but collapsed.

Snow scrambled up the bank. He did a quick back and forth with his head, an instant scan of the scene. Pook was on the ground, moaning, his shotgun out of reach on the ground beside him.

Snow picked up the shotgun and tossed it away. Snow put his boot on Pook and gave him a shove with it. Pook rolled from his side onto his back.

"Lilly!" Snow called.

The white police truck pulled up and stopped, and Stanley Beans hopped out. Snow gave him a wave, a *get over here* kind of wave.

"Stanley! Check on JJ here. I think he's hit. I'm going for Lilly," Snow added and began to walk away.

"What about him?" Stanley said, pointing at Pook.

"Check him, too. He's hit bad," Snow said.

Snow began to trot upriver along the upper edge of the cutback. He saw Chubby's plane on the beach a half mile or so upriver. He saw Chubby in his brown battered bomber jacket on the beach heading this direction. As if he was out for a stroll. Snow gave him a wave with his arm over his head.

"Lilly! Lilly! It's me. It's okay! You can come out!" Snow hollered as loud as he could.

He kept walking upriver, then he saw a head pop up from the long grass.

"Lilly! It's okay, it's over!" shouted Snow.

Lilly stood. Within seconds, they were in each other's arms.

They both stood there and hugged each other swaying back and forth, not saying anything. Lilly was crying. Snow was too—the relief pouring out of him in his tears.

Lilly pulled her head back and looked up at Snow. "I'm pregnant," she said.

Snow was confused. He was wondering what Lilly had been through, worrying that she had been raped. Lilly saw his confusion.

"I did not get raped, Brady. You made it just in time. The plane helped," she said.

"You're pregnant. I am so happy. We're going to have a baby?" Snow said.

"Yup," she said, smiling at him.

"I love you. All my heart," he whispered in her ear.

"I love you, too," she said.

Lilly saw the other plane first and said, "Look!" and pointed as the blue trooper plane floated by them. It flew close enough that they could clearly see the pilot. Lilly and Snow both waved at the pilot, Trooper Debbie Roop and she wagged her wings. The plane looped around to survey the scene, then landed on the beach below them.

Lilly and Snow stayed in an embrace as they watched the plane land. They saw Trooper Dick get out of the passenger side and run toward them. He had never seen Trooper Dick run, or even walk fast. He laughed, wincing from the pain in his arm.

"You're bleeding. You've been hit," Lilly said.

"Just a pellet wound," Snow said. "I'll be fine."

Trooper Dick made a loop by the cabin but was only there for a minute before he met Lilly and Snow.

"Lilly!" Trooper Dick said, gasping. "Lilly, you alright?" he asked her and put his hand on her shoulder. At that moment, Snow knew that Trooper Dick loved Lilly. But he understood it was like the love of a father toward his daughter, his baby girl. Trooper Dick had tears in his eyes, which was even more of a surprise than his running. Snow thought all the love and emotion for Trooper Dick was snuffed out long ago, like it had been drowned in the bathtub by the job. He was glad to be wrong.

Chief Snow took his left arm off of Lilly and opened it up, inviting Trooper Dick into the circle for a group hug.

Trooper Debbie came up over the bank. Snow and Trooper Dick both pulled an arm out of the group hug, leaving a space for her to walk right into the group embrace.

"I am okay, Richard," Lilly said to Trooper Dick. Everyone understood that she was calling him Richard as a term of endearment.

"I got beat up a little bit, but that is all," she said. Trooper Dick pulled his head back, searching for her eyes, hugging her again.

"How about you, Chief? Hey, you're bleeding," said Trooper Dick.

"Can I have that hat lying on the beach?" Snow said with a smile. Trooper Dick put his hand on his head; he didn't even know his hat was gone.

Snow disengaged from the group a bit and lifted his left arm to take a look. He had been hit near his left elbow, and once in his vest, but it didn't penetrate through it. The blood from his wound near his elbow had run down the inside of his shirt and was dripping off his hand.

"Just a scratch," he said.

"I need to look at that. Better go to the clinic, I think," Lilly said.

Trooper Dick was the first to break the hug and get back to business. Meanwhile, Stanley was waving and hollering.

"We got a lot going on here. I will handle the crime scene. Pook is dead, I'm sure you know. Stanley needs some help with JJ who is injured," Trooper Dick said.

"I think JJ got hit when Pook was shooting at me. He needs medical attention," Snow said.

"I can look at him," Lilly said.

"No, we got this. I need to get to work here, and I need you and Chief Snow to get to the clinic and get looked at. We got this," Trooper Dick said.

At that moment, Chubby appeared over the cut bank, grinning. "Have no fear, Chubby is here!"

Troopers Dick and Debbie left to go see about the crime scene.

"I thought I maybe got Pook, but he shot up my plane, so I guess not. When I saw him with the shotgun, I came as close as I possibly could. I feel like my wing may have brushed the cabin," Chubby said.

Snow gave Chubby a quick break down of what happened from his point of view.

"When you buzzed the cabin, it gave me a chance to make a break for it. I could be dead, if you did not do that," Lilly said, her voice cracking and raspy with emotion.

"Lilly, my dear, I would have flown my plane through hell if I thought it would help you in any way." Chubby gave Lilly a courtly bow.

"We are in your debt, my friend. I think your flying saved the day," Snow said.

"My pleasure. I gotta see about my plane, now. We are burning daylight!"

CHAPTER 17
THIRD TIME LUCKY

The troopers had a lot of things to do and were busy. Pook's body had to be processed, as well as the entire crime scene. Two planes on the beach needed to be moved. People needed to get to the clinic. Interviews had to happen as soon as possible. There were a lot of moving parts, but these two knew their business and handled things with aplomb. Chief Snow was happy not to have to direct traffic revolving around the incident.

He had gotten stitched up and was waiting for Lilly to come out of the clinic. He had an inspiration and went over to the AC Store. When he came back, Lilly was out of the exam room and was chatting with staff. She saw him enter and noticed Snow carrying a red heart shaped box with a card on it.

Lilly approached Snow in the lobby and said, "What's that?"

At the same time, Troopers Dick and Debbie came in the clinic. But Snow and Lilly were focused only on each other. The troopers froze in place as they saw what looked to be some kind of moment happening between Lilly and Snow.

Chief Snow said, "Open the card." He noticed that several of Lilly's clinic co-workers were watching them. It was a Valentine's Day card, as Snow had grabbed the first card he could get.

Inside the card was written, *Marry me?* inside a big hand-drawn heart.

Snow got down on one knee right there in the clinic. He could hear some excited whispers coming from the women watching.

"Lilly. You are the love of my life. I am nothing without you! Will you marry me?" Snow stammered.

Lilly reached out for Snow's hand and raised him to his feet. They embraced and she said, "Yes of course, silly!"

Snow picked her up and the women behind cheered and clapped.

"Hey, be careful. I am pregnant, you know!"

Trooper Dick came over and smacked Snow hard on the back. But he spoke to Lilly. "You're pregnant? Wow, congratulations, Lilly!"

"Thank you, Richard," Lilly said, and they all realized this was going to be her thing now.

"Yes. Thank you, Richard," Snow said with a smirk. Trooper Debbie gave a smile of appreciation.

"Hey, you need to keep this lady out of harm's way, Snow. She's pregnant, you know!" Trooper Dick said.

■ ■ ■

Back at the Round House, Snow and Lilly sat chatting on the red and green sofa. They had come from an emergency council meeting and were talking about what had transpired.

"I think they're probably right, you know," she said to Snow. "It may be complicated to stay here after this. I mean, no one blames you for shooting Pook. Yet. But later, some of his family may have issues with it. I don't know," she said, trailing off.

"Did you know Pook's wife, Nancy, actually thanked me?"

Snow said. "She looked like a weight had been lifted off her, and her face looked clear, you know?"

"I didn't know that, but I am not surprised. He was very cruel toward her," Lilly said.

"I don't see why we should have to leave. Pook was to blame for all of this, and he got what he deserved. Why should we leave?" Snow said.

"You heard what the mayor said. We don't *have* to leave. He just thought it may be best for everybody. I think he was being wise, don't you? Annie Blue and the others will support you and me if we stay, but I think they are right. It is probably better for everyone if we take this opportunity to leave Togiak. I know you don't feel like we should have to, but in your heart, you know it's best, I think," Lilly said.

"I am being stubborn, I suppose. But I have invested so much in this place. It seems so sudden to just pack up and leave. And where are we going to go, and what are we going to do?" Snow said.

The earsplitting sound of the old phone ringing pierced the air. Snow jumped up like he was shot out of a cannon and snatched the phone. He thought he got to it in time, but the phone made an odd, single *ding* sound as he picked it up.

"Hello."

"Please hold for Senator Begich," a woman's voice said.

"Please hold for Senator Begich," Snow said to Lilly, making a face.

"Tom, I mean, your highness. What's up?" Snow said when Begich came on the line.

"I heard you may be looking for work. I hope you will consider what we talked about in Anchorage," Begich said.

"I am listening," Snow said. He was looking at Lilly, and she was looking back at him.